Praise for *She D...*

"Tiffany communicates clearly that dreams look different for each and every woman; and no matter what her background, losses, or standing may be, she is not to be silenced or dismissed but to rise up to take her place because it is her birthright to dream. This is a message she lives, inspiring us with her bold faith and her capacity to encourage us collectively to make a difference where we are, with what we have."

—**Ashley Abercrombie**, podcast cohost of *Why Tho* and author of *The Rise of the Truth Teller* (forthcoming)

"Tiffany is full of fire and life. She writes, and more importantly, lives this book. She's got grit, passion, and a depth that causes you to read each word and see that you were born to live out your dreams while there is still breath in your lungs. Her words will cause you to see that you're stronger than you know and created for more."

—**Andi Andrew**, author of *She Is Free*, speaker, pastor, and founder of She Is Free

"Persistent hope jumps off every page of Tiffany Bluhm's beautiful book, *She Dreams*. From the overcoming of adversity within her own life to the stories of biblical heroes whose broken lives were pieced together by the God of redemption, readers will find courage to let their own dreams take root, knowing that there is no tragedy, misstep, or disappointment that God can't redeem. Whether you are single or married, with or without children, working in the home or outside of it, Bluhm reminds all of us that the Lord wants to use your passions, skills, and dreams for his purposes and glory."

—**Katelyn Beaty**, author of *A Woman's Place: A Christian Vision for Your Calling in the Office, the Home, and the World* and former managing editor of *Christianity Today*

"Tiffany speaks with the conviction and experience of a woman twice her age. She shares honestly about the cost, sacrifice, and grit required to not only see your dreams come true but also lift others to reach theirs."
—**Eric Boles**, author of *Moving to Great* and president of The Game Changers Inc.

"Tiffany is thoughtful, clear-headed, and filled with rich biblical insight. These same qualities shine in her most recent book, *She Dreams*, where she explores how one's best instincts, aspirations, and hopes can become a reality. I found myself praying through my own discarded dreams, inviting God to breathe life into them again; I know the same will be true for you."
—**Bryan Halferty**, lead pastor of Anchor Church, Tacoma, WA

"This book is for the dreamers and for the women who are so buried in their season of life that they have forgotten to dream. Tiffany beautifully reminds us all that we are created to do big things and that no dream is too big. Empowered by examples from Scripture and her own life, Tiffany speaks encouragement and truth, emphasizing the need to just START and take the first step toward your dream."
—**Nickie Snyder**, podcast host of *The Things She Does* and cardiac nurse practitioner

Live the Life You Were Created For

She DREAMS

Tiffany Bluhm

ABINGDON WOMEN / NASHVILLE

SHE DREAMS
LIVE THE LIFE YOU WERE CREATED FOR

Library of Congress Cataloging-in-Publication Data has been requested.

ISBN 978-1-5018-7832-9

19 20 21 22 23 24 25 26 27 28—10 9 8 7 6 5 4 3 2 1
MANUFACTURED IN THE UNITED STATES OF AMERICA

Contents

Introduction ix

She Dreams Declaration xiii

1. You Were Born for This 3

2. Broken Dreams 21

3. Rewarding Life and Rewarding Work 37

4. Tell Me Why 55

5. Haters Gonna Hate 73

6. Good Ole Days. 89

7. Dust Yourself Off. 111

8. Get Your Head Out of the Sand. 127

9. Stop Scrolling and Start Rolling 145

10. Voice of Truth 159

11. Refresh Yourself. 175

12. Destiny. 191

Notes 203

To all the women who dream, persist, fight, and slay:
this one is for you.

Introduction

"Never give up on your dreams, my darling, for they
are your birthright, and you owe it to the world to
become the Queen, you are."

— Mark Anthony[1]

Above my bed hangs a gold metal frame with a message that reads
"Breathing dreams like air." It's a line from F. Scott Fitzgerald's classic
work *The Great Gatsby*, and it's the first thing I see when I walk into my
room and the last thing I see before I crawl into bed each night. The
words are a reminder that my dreams are necessary to me—not apart
from me, but vital to me. I can't escape my dreams. They are with me
wherever I go. We coexist. I inhale them, however small or big, and
remember that I am built for something bigger than myself. I am built
to glorify God, to partner with Him for a beautiful (albeit messy at
times) life.

That bold statement was hung above my bed at a time when I
dreamed wild, God-sized dreams and yet there was no evidence of my
dreams becoming my reality. Still, years later, here I sit at my dining
room table, savoring all God has done in my life since that message

first made its way into my room. I have not given up on trusting the Dream Giver and He has not given up on me.

You and I were created to dream. More than the dream of becoming homecoming queen (although who doesn't want to wear a crown), or owning that rare purebred dog you love (if you are the dog lovin' type), or running that marathon (bless you), or starting that veggie garden (yum), you and I were born, destined, and purposed to dream wild, audacious, make-your-heart race, only-God-could-really-bring-this-to-pass kind of dreams. It doesn't matter if you are practical or impractical, young or old, rich or poor, you have the capacity to dream big dreams, without excuse.

If you still have a pulse, then God is not done with you, even if you feel like He is. You have more life to live, more ground to cover, more stories to tell, more songs to sing. You have more. Neither you nor I have fully arrived. We are growing, changing into the women God destined us to be as we chase after Him and draw near to His heart.

In addition to sharing stories of women from the past and present as well as my own life experiences, I'll be inviting us to look to the story of a biblical dreamer—one dedicated to the dreams of God—who offers us inspiration and guidance as we pursue our own God-sized dreams. Moses, one of the most famous characters of the Old Testament, was an ordinary person like you and me who listened to God, leaned into God's will, and partnered with God for big, glorious dreams. As we uncover themes from his story that provide vision and clarity for our own dreams and combine those with the examples and inspiration of contemporary women, you'll discover what it takes to identify, embrace, and pursue the dreams that the Divine has for *you*. I'll also invite you to consider how your dreams can take shape through practices such as reflecting, collaborating, lifelong learning, pursuing passion, counting the cost, praying, holding on to hope, and trusting God for the deepest desires of your heart. (And if you want to make the journey with a group of girlfriends, a separate study guide and DVD are also available.)

As you drink in the message of this book from the first page to the last, I hope you find yourself in the story as a woman who is an overcomer, a woman who is brave and courageous, a woman who doesn't give up easily—because when you pursue your dreams and live the life you were created for, you bring heaven to earth. You rehearse heaven in your season because you have trusted God, the Dream Giver, for your victory.

So from one dreamer to another, may you rise up to take your place, because no one will make all your dreams come true. No one is going to hold up a silver platter with your sweet dreams on it. I do wish life was that simple, but you and I both know it most certainly is not. To see your dreams become reality demands a partnership with the Divine, the One who knows you inside and out. It requires a mammoth amount of patience, incredible trust, and immense hope that God will do all that He has said He will do. Your dreams may not turn out exactly as you planned; they may just turn out better and sweeter and more glorious than you ever could have believed possible. I hope they do. I hope that at the end of your days you stand before the King, the Dream Giver, and celebrate a life well lived, a life well dreamed. May this book be a guide, a compass, or maybe even a kick in the pants for you to answer the call of your Dream Giver because, sister, you were created to dream!

Tiffany

She Dreams Declaration

She dreams of sunlight, strong winds, and victory.
She dreams of a majestic story, a whimsical mystery.

She dreams of life abundant, so free and wild.
She dreams of the Father's call to her, "Beloved child."

She dreams of slaying dragons, saving the day,
She dreams of taking her place, at the feet of Yahweh.

She dreams in vivid colors, jewel tones, and pastels.
She dreams of freedom and truth, like the clangs of the
Liberty Bell.

She dreams of teaching, leading, and serving.
She dreams of a journey of which she is deserving.

She dreams of grace, mercy, and hope.
She dreams of thriving not just learning to cope.

She dreams of rushing peace like a river.
She dreams of the one and only Dream Giver.

—Tiffany Bluhm

1

You Were Born for This

1

You Were Born for This

Do you ever look at someone who has achieved something great and think, "She was born to do that"? We look at Deborah in the Book of Judges; Queen Esther; Mary, the mother of Jesus; Joan of Arc, Eleanor Roosevelt; Harriet Tubman; Frida Kahlo; Mother Teresa; Margaret Thatcher; Serena Williams; or Joanna Gaines and we are in awe of who each woman is, what she has overcome, and what she has achieved. We think to ourselves, *Snaaap, she is KILLING it! She is one wise and powerful woman.*

As we think about women who have defied the odds and pursued their dreams, we can sometimes assume, perhaps subconsciously, that those marvelous women possess some sort of special "unicorn powers" or superpower gifts that you and I would never have access to. The truth is, the women that you and I admire, both past and present, have a beating heart just like ours. Each one of them has or has had insecurities, fears, and setbacks just like you and me. The one thing we know for sure of each woman that we look up to is this: *she dreams.*

She dreams impossible dreams. She fights to see them come to pass, and she doesn't take no for an answer when it comes to the fulfillment of those dreams. She believes she was created to dream; and dear friend, so are you and I.

No matter who you are or where you've come from, no matter how many Benjamins you have in your bank account or mothballs you have in your pockets, no matter how bold you are or how shy, no matter how perfect your pedigree or how sketchy your past—you, lovely one, were born for a lifetime of beauty and hope. Within you are unlimited dreams to pursue as you live your wild life. You are here on purpose for a purpose. No matter the details surrounding the story of your birth or beginnings (trust me on this one), you were born to dream of a better, sweeter, fairer existence for you and the world around you.

Other folks may say you are a screwup. Your parents might think you are crazy as a box of rocks (a common expression in my home, thanks to a popular children's movie), or you might believe the nonsense that you are just here to live your ordinary life. Quiet. Inconsequential. Never making waves. Never pushing back. Never raising a ruckus. Never chasing after the next best thing.

Well, sister, I'm not buying it. I've read a book on it, and from Genesis to Revelation I've discovered that you and I were built to dream about the impossible, the out of reach, the beautiful, the lovely, the someday, the not yet. We were created to dream about things that matter, things that spark joy—to find ways to serve others, ways that push us to our limits, ways that help us face our insecurities and hang-ups. *All of it.*

Hear me now: the Dream Giver—the One who built us, created us, handcrafted us—chose to entrust us with gifts, skills, and abilities that are unique to each of us. Even when those precious skills and gifts of yours aren't activated in a particular season of life, it doesn't mean they aren't yours. It doesn't mean the One who gave them to you has taken them away. It doesn't mean they are worthless and can never be used for any good work. Our God is so very good to us. He is a Giver of good gifts; and when He gives a gift, He knows the power and magnitude the gift has. We, His beloved and cherished daughters, must unwrap each gift and use it. How and when we use our gifts is important, but first and foremost, we must recognize that we were created to dream.

You Do You

So many of us are built for far more than we may be doing in this season, and that is okay. What is not okay is denying our longing to do more at some point in our lives. I recently listened to a podcast about a woman who experienced restlessness when her kids were little. She thought her days were lovely overall and she adored her children and being a mother, but she felt that something was missing. I've felt that rub as well, and I know I'm not alone. I've talked to countless women—with and without children, single and married—who long to do something "bigger" despite whatever busy or barren season they currently find themselves in. I've also talked to women whose lives seem "big" by the world's standards yet feel they are missing out on the truly important everyday experiences of life and home. Wherever you find yourself, you may find that your day-to-day reality no longer excites you in the way it used to and you know deep in your heart that you are ready for something different—some kind of change that will renew and energize you. The woman on the podcast discovered she was made to create and now finds deep satisfaction in her work as a calligrapher. I teared up as she shared about her business that has expanded over the years.

The truth is that every woman is stronger than she thinks she is and built for rewarding work—whether that work is inside or outside the home. I have found this to be true in my own life. Once upon a time, when I was up all hours of the night with a colicky eight-week-old, I launched a little blog. I called it *Learn How to Mom* because my husband always joked that I was literally "learning how to mom" with one newly adopted three-year-old from Uganda and one squishy little baby fresh from my womb (who left me with such a sea of stretch marks on my belly that I'm tempted not to even consider anything but an arctic parka when I go swimming in public). I wrote on and on about life as a mama, giving suggestions for how not to lose your sanity when your baby has a blow-out in one of those fancy-pants baby carriers at the grocery store when you know that folks are already looking at you and thinking you could use a shower yourself.

I had always wanted to write poignant pieces that would inspire others to live the life God had designed for them, and I decided it was time. Why that led me to talk about life with little ones was beyond me, but that was my season; and I thought to myself that if the Lord was good enough to show me Himself in that crazy but wonderful season of my life, then I might as well share His encouragement with others.

I decided that even if my audience turned out to be just two of my girlfriends, I would write. I wrote every chance I could. In my season of zero to little sleep, often choosing to write instead of showering or doing dishes, I lovingly and often frantically typed my tale of how I was holding on to God's goodness and grace through all of the celebrations and challenges—especially the discouraging times. I would lie awake in bed with a laptop computer atop my blankets, hammering away on the keys as I wrote about experiences and emotions that I believed needed to be shared. All day long I would scribble ideas on envelopes that most likely held a bill I needed to pay or on crumpled paper towels left beside the sink. I am the first to admit these blogs were…well…as the cool kids say, "basic." Again, I was operating on very little sleep and most certainly was clocking my ten thousand hours; but friend, I did not lack conviction. In fact, I was full of it. Conviction and passion kept me focused. (This is when I discovered my undying love for coffee. Pure coincidence, of course.)

Each of our souls is built for more than we can possibly imagine; and pursuing our God-given dreams, however big or small they may seem, opens us to a bright and shining life of meaning and purpose.

So after birthing my own baby, I also birthed a blog and a full-time job; and my husband and I had recently bought a new house that needed all sorts of renovating. It was not the time to be dreaming about new ventures, but I knew I would be like a dying star if I didn't pursue them. You see, I deeply believe each of our souls is built for more than we can possibly imagine; and pursuing our God-given dreams, however big or small they may seem, opens us to a bright and shining life of meaning and purpose.

I know I'm a better person—which for me includes being a better wife and mama—when I first connect with the Lord and then do what I believe I was uniquely created to do. The same concept applies to you: when you are *killing* it at whatever it is you slay, there is a chance you feel most like yourself—the *you* that you know deep down in your bones God made you to be.

I hope you are hearing me, dear one. May you never let your dreams, however possible or impossible they may seem, pass you by without grit, a big ol' heart, and a whole lot of humility. Now, I do not mean to confuse contentment in Christ with pursuing your dreams. Rather, as we abide in Christ, He stirs us to act, dream, create, and do. The Dream Giver calls us, leads us, speaks to us, restores us, heals us, fulfills us, and entrusts us with dreams.

My kids' favorite book, *The Plans I Have for You*, says it like this,

> You are my hands and my feet there on Earth.
> I've given you a purpose—it's been there since birth![1]

So if you are a painter, bust out the brushes. If you are a writer, sharpen that pencil or get out that computer. If you are a runner, grab those nifty running shoes. If you are a singer, then saaang, girrrl. If you are a helper, start helping. If you are a giver, give generously. If you are a peacemaker, build bridges toward peace. Do what makes you uniquely you! You do you, friend. No one else can. You'll never regret doing what you love—unless it's illegal or harmful. That would be bad. Go ahead and regret that—or better yet, don't do it. But if something sparks joy in you and blesses others, then go ahead and get at it! Because you, my darling, were created to pursue the dreams of your heart.

Your Past Won't Break You

Many of us feel our past mistakes disqualify us from opportunities, promotions, and second chances; but I propose that no matter who you are or what you've experienced, the screams of failure, grief, and defeat tucked in your mind will not break you and might be the making of you, proving to be quite handy as you dream impossible dreams. I've found this to be true in my own life.

In 1986, I was abandoned at birth. At two days old, without a mother to nurse me or a father to rock me to sleep, I was left in a home for orphaned children and became one of twenty-five million orphans in India. Trust me on this one: abandoned in your most vulnerable moment will make you question if you are valuable, let alone valuable enough to do something great.

In 1994, a little girl in my third-grade class told me we couldn't be friends because my skin was dirty and brown. It was the first time I ever wept over the color of my skin. It felt wrong to simply be me. I was judged by the color of my skin and not the content of my character. It wasn't the last time someone would remind me I was different and didn't belong, but it was the first; and that first experience of prejudice made me question if I fit in this world.

In 2007, I moved to Manchester, England, to pursue a relationship with a tall English gentleman I met at a summer wedding and with whom I fell in love. I never dreamed I would one day grow up and move six thousand miles from home to be with the man of my dreams. He was everything I hoped for. After I quit my job and booked a one-way ticket to England, you can imagine my surprise when Prince Charming informed me three days after making the move, "Tiffany, I have no desire for you." Mic drop. I left his house and didn't know whether to go left or right to get back to my place. Through tears I wandered the streets of Manchester looking for my way back home so I could weep in private. From that experience I wondered if I was capable of making any good choices for myself.

Actually, I did make a good choice, and I married my husband, Derek, in 2009. Then in 2013, after a two-year adoption process, we traveled to Uganda to meet our son, Lucius, who was twelve months old at the time—born to another woman but birthed in my heart. His mother hemorrhaged to death after giving birth to him, and he was placed in a children's home at three days old. For three months, I held him, cuddled him, and let his little laughs seep into every corner of my heart. A week before our court date, in which I would become his legal guardian, we were informed that due to unforeseen circumstances we would no longer be able to adopt him. With a nursery ready at home and his name tattooed on my heart, I kissed his forehead and said good-bye knowing I would never see him again.

Each of these experiences has deeply affected my outlook on life and love. They are my series of unfortunate events. My past experiences, stacked on top of one another, add up to some heartache. Aching defeat. I would be lying if I didn't admit they affected how I viewed myself. At times, I felt that my past experiences would prohibit my opportunity to be loved, lead others, have a family, or see my dreams come true. Our hard moments and pain become a filter we see through, causing our feelings of doubt, shame, and loss to shape our view of the world and everyone in it.

Our messy moments aren't the defining line of our story. They are merely twists in the narrative.

We do our best to hush the screams of failure, defeat, or grief, but perhaps within those experiences is our greatest asset. A tension to be managed, not ignored. Our pain, if we lean into it, will teach us endurance. We'll discover that we are stronger than we think we are and that what God has for us will not pass us by because of our past. Our messy moments aren't the defining line of our story. They are merely twists in the narrative. You and I must never believe the lie that the dark days will dampen the bright ones to come.

The *New Yorker* published an article on what it means to be resilient, and it boils down to this: "Frame adversity as a challenge, and you become more flexible and able to deal with it, move on, learn from it, and grow. Focus on it, frame it as a threat, and a potentially traumatic event becomes an enduring problem; you become more inflexible, and more likely to be negatively affected."[2] You see, how we perceive our past difficulties matters.

The honest-to-goodness truth is that each of us seeks a new ending to the broken storyline of our lives. We either look for others to fix our broken pieces, or we look to our accomplishments or work to make us feel better; but none will satisfy. No external force will fix our inner brokenness. Only Jesus, by His grace and goodness, can tenderly sustain us—and eventually heal us.

The Making of You

As our Good Companion sustains us and begins the process of healing, we can allow our pain to be a teacher, making us into the women we are meant to be. I learned this through each of the painful experiences I shared.

Working through my abandonment issues provided an intimate communion with my own frailty, and my hunger for love and acceptance was—and continues to be—satisfied in Jesus. Eight years ago I was able to visit the orphanage where I was left and found that no answer to any of my burning questions would ever fix me. Knowing that Jesus loves me would be what calmed my questioning heart, not facts. As Christ healed my abandoned heart, my understanding of loss grew within me compassion for the left behind and the underserved. I would not trade that for the world. It has undoubtedly shaped the way I love people.

The Lord really decided to show off a year ago when the woman who ran the orphanage and took me in at two days old tracked me down. She was in the States visiting family and found me through mutual friends I had no idea we shared. I met her and heard how she felt deeply compelled to care for a baby and then her burning desire was met when a newborn was placed in her arms. She loved me as her own. After hearing that story I discovered that peace can be applied retroactively. Experiences you and I had ten, twenty, or even forty years ago can be rewritten as we allow hope to rise from our broken memories.

Working through my ongoing experience of discrimination has taught me to never let someone else define my worth, no matter how powerful they may appear. No one has the power to define me or you without our consent. It doesn't matter who they are, the color of their skin, or the wealth and privilege they lord over us. Discrimination has deep roots of fear, and the only thing that can put fear in its place is love. First John 4:18 (NIV) tells us, "There is no fear in love. But perfect love drives out fear, because fear has to do with punishment. The one who fears is not made perfect in love." Someone may do their best to rob us of opportunity or convince us that we're disqualified because of our skin or gender or age or any other distinguishing characteristic, but they can never define the value of our souls. The Author of Love settled that score long ago.

Working through my experience with Prince Charming taught me that I am enough. Although my childhood feelings of abandonment and rejection were amplified as Prince Charming called it quits, I discovered no one could fulfill me but the King. The Englishman wasn't going to fix what was broken whether he stayed with me or left me. As I healed from my heartache, I didn't expect a prospective suitor to throw me out with the garbage or be my king. I would not allow a man to have that kind of power over me. I approached potential relationships with a heart to share my life with someone who loved Christ and who would care for me. At the time of this writing, I've been married to Derek for nearly ten years. I am so very grateful for Prince Charming's unfortunate exit from my life because of the lessons I learned. Lessons accessible only through the pain of heartbreak. While we may prefer to avoid pain and loss, it can make way for beauty and redemption we never thought possible.

Working through losing Lucius taught me that love, not DNA, makes a family and that it is always worth the fight to place the lonely in families. While my husband and I did not come home with Lucius, we did come home with Jericho, who was two-and-a-half years old when he joined our little family. In the Old Testament, Jericho was the first city God promised to His chosen people. As our first child, we thought it fitting to name him after the gift God gave to His people. Both Jericho and I were left in vulnerable moments, but together we make a family. Love is a powerful force that squelches the flames of shame and rejection and makes room for belonging and significance. Love makes way for truth and vision over lies and confusion.

Four years ago when I had my biological son, one of my own flesh and blood, I met the first person I've ever shared DNA with. He has my eyes and my natural hair. I'm Indian, and there are literally a billion of us, but this Indian lives in my home and calls me mama. My past experience of abandonment gave me a hunger for a healthy family.

I share all of this to say that my past failures and experiences gave me opportunities for personal growth I would not have had otherwise, and I've had the honor to share what I've learned about the companionship and redemptive ways of Jesus with others through my ministry of writing and speaking. My painful experiences truly have been the making of me, not the breaking of me.

The human experience is not easy, yet deep in our pain there are lessons to be learned and strength to be gained. We must reassess the limitations and disqualifications we've come to accept in our lives if we are to be women who dream God-sized dreams. Our adversity may quite possibly be the source of our greatest assets—our crown jewels, if you will. Adversity shapes us, molds us, and makes us the brave, resilient, beautiful souls we are intended to be.

Bigger Than Us

Sometimes the dreams of God become our own when we least expect it. We may be discontent or living a life we love, and all the while the Lord is preparing our hearts for even greater things than we can imagine. We may not sense it, but He is setting the stage for something glorious, wondrous, and perhaps even downright terrifying.

Moses, a hero of the Old Testament, knew a thing or two about God-sized dreams. Like us, he was chosen for great and mighty plans before he was even born. The Lord placed him in Egypt on purpose for a purpose. Moses would foreshadow the coming King who would redeem us all. When he was growing up, I bet Moses had no idea of all God planned. Before we see Moses do extraordinary things in the name of justice and freedom, we see his rocky beginning, the place where all good stories start. We read about those beginnings in Exodus 1 and 2:

^{1:8}*Eventually, a new king came to power in Egypt who knew nothing about Joseph or what he had done. ⁹He said to his people, "Look, the people of Israel now outnumber us and are stronger than we are. ¹⁰We must make a plan to keep them from growing even more. If we don't, and if war breaks out, they will join our enemies and fight against us. Then they will escape from the country."*

¹¹*So the Egyptians made the Israelites their slaves. They appointed brutal slave drivers over them, hoping to wear them down with crushing labor. They forced them to build the cities of Pithom and Rameses as supply centers for the king. ¹²But the more the Egyptians oppressed them, the more the Israelites multiplied and spread, and the more alarmed the Egyptians became. ¹³So the Egyptians worked the people of Israel without mercy. ¹⁴They made their lives bitter, forcing them to mix mortar and make bricks and do all the work in the fields. They were ruthless in all their demands.*

¹⁵*Then Pharaoh, the king of Egypt, gave this order to the Hebrew midwives, Shiphrah and Puah: ¹⁶"When you help the Hebrew women as they give birth, watch as they deliver. If the baby is a boy, kill him; if it is a girl, let her live." ¹⁷But because the midwives feared God, they refused to obey the king's orders. They allowed the boys to live, too.*

¹⁸*So the king of Egypt called for the midwives. "Why have you done this?" he demanded. "Why have you allowed the boys to live?"*

¹⁹*"The Hebrew women are not like the Egyptian women," the midwives replied. "They are more vigorous and have their babies so quickly that we cannot get there in time."*

²⁰*So God was good to the midwives, and the Israelites continued to multiply, growing more and more powerful.*

²¹And because the midwives feared God, he gave them families of their own.

²²Then Pharaoh gave this order to all his people: "Throw every newborn Hebrew boy into the Nile River. But you may let the girls live."

❧ ❧ ❧

²:¹About this time, a man and woman from the tribe of Levi got married. ²The woman became pregnant and gave birth to a son. She saw that he was a special baby and kept him hidden for three months. ³But when she could no longer hide him, she got a basket made of papyrus reeds and waterproofed it with tar and pitch. She put the baby in the basket and laid it among the reeds along the bank of the Nile River. ⁴The baby's sister then stood at a distance, watching to see what would happen to him.

⁵Soon Pharaoh's daughter came down to bathe in the river, and her attendants walked along the riverbank. When the princess saw the basket among the reeds, she sent her maid to get it for her. ⁶When the princess opened it, she saw the baby. The little boy was crying, and she felt sorry for him. "This must be one of the Hebrew children," she said.

⁷Then the baby's sister approached the princess. "Should I go and find one of the Hebrew women to nurse the baby for you?" she asked.

⁸"Yes, do!" the princess replied. So the girl went and called the baby's mother.

⁹"Take this baby and nurse him for me," the princess told the baby's mother. "I will pay you for your help." So the woman took her baby home and nursed him.

> ¹⁰*Later, when the boy was older, his mother brought him back to Pharaoh's daughter, who adopted him as her own son. The princess named him Moses, for she explained, "I lifted him out of the water."*
>
> *(Exodus 1:8–2:10)*

It is heartbreaking to think of a mama laying her baby in a basket and sending him down a river in hopes he'll be rescued rather than die at the hands of evil, jealous men. Yet in His power and sovereignty God not only spared Moses' life but also had a plan for his life—from before he was even born. Like Jeremiah, who was set apart to be a prophet to the nations before his birth (Jeremiah 1:5), it is evident that God's hand was on Moses' life from day one.

Now, when your story begins in societal turmoil in a time when the haves and the have-nots are clearly defined, a time when the murder of baby boys is the order of the day, a time when discrimination is at an all-time high, your "normal" might not be healthy or life-giving. Your reality might be harmful to you and those around you, but it is all you know. Yet your steps are still guided by a divine hand.

The Egyptians who enslaved the Hebrew people raised Moses, who was chosen by God. As a royal he had the riches of earth, but God planned for him to live a life not of ease and riches but of sacrifice. God's plans and dreams for Moses, tucked in that baby in a basket, would change everything, not only for him but also for God's people of his day and generations to come.

I wonder if Moses had a clear sense that God had a mighty grip on his life. Or perhaps, like us, he found himself swept up into a story bigger than himself, authored by God for his good and not his demise. Perhaps he realized over time that God's miraculous ways would supersede any human plans or way of life he knew. But first he was just an innocent baby found in a basket on the riverbank.

You and I may not fully understand all that God has been working in and through us since our birth, but make no mistake, *He is working.* God has plans for us that won't be stopped. Why? Because He made us on purpose for a purpose.

2
Broken Dreams

2

Broken Dreams

It's mortifying to watch the ice queen slip on the ice during her triple axel, triple toe move. It's devastating when our dear friend suffers through a miscarriage, and it's awful when the friend who worked with blood, sweat, and tears for her dream job is demoted for reasons she couldn't have foreseen. But when it's our dreams that are crushed, it's earth-shattering. It's draining and sometimes devastating to see the best-laid plans fall apart right in front of our eyes. No one plans for their dreams to fall apart or shatter in front of them when the glorious end is in sight, but it happens to the best of us. We can do what we know is right and things can still crash and burn, but even in the broken moments there is a pathway where everything that's broken can be made whole.

Though we're just getting off the ground with this whole business of chasing our dreams, the reality is that sometimes our initial dreams are shattered before God's better, sweeter, life-giving dreams can come to pass. It's one thing to address our own internal brokenness (as we did in the previous chapter), but it's another thing entirely to experience broken dreams, which can derail us. Broken dreams often usher in dark nights, stormy thoughts, and a sense of hopelessness that only God can redeem. It happened to Moses, and it happens to us.

Faced with Our Powerlessness

Broken dreams, no matter how they happen, can cause us to question our worth, our direction, and even our right to embrace a God-sized dream. Many of us, myself included, sometimes feel that our plans are downright foolproof. Nothing will go wrong because we are always one step ahead and think everything through. It will all turn out rosy because life is rainbows and unicorns. Until it doesn't.

I have a tendency to be pretty positive and am flabbergasted when things don't go as planned, which is nearly every day of my life since I have children and bills and an actual life. Yet more often than not, I believe nothing will disrupt the course of my dreams. *My plan is perfect,* I tell myself, only to witness my perfect plans shattered because I, in fact, am not supremely in charge of every living thing. Although I own a coffee cup that says otherwise. Okay, I own several coffee cups that would lead you to believe mama is in charge. All lies.

Despite the outcomes of our plan, God can redeem our broken dreams—replacing them with even better ones—and set us on solid ground for the future. Even if those dreams have been dead for days, months, or years, the Lord is faithful to hear us when we call. Some of us may find ourselves in situations where we've lost more than we ever imagined at the hands of someone else's selfish choices. It can be easy to throw up a fist at God and ask Him why such a tragedy would happen; but on this side of heaven in a broken world where there is sin and suffering, unspeakable tragedy seems to find us in one way or another. Some say that you are either in a season of suffering, have just left a season of suffering, or are headed into a season of suffering.

Suffering finds us all, and the sharp pain of shattered dreams can make us wonder if God has a plan at all—or if He does have a plan, if it is good. The Scriptures remind us that suffering and trials will always be part of this life but that we can take heart because God has overcome the world (John 16:33). We can trust Him and do what only we can do.

Though our dreams may be broken, our attitude and actions are still in our control. Who we decide to be and what we decide to believe in the wake of broken dreams can determine our steps to see them made whole again. If we believe God has failed us, we'll act like it. If we believe God is for us, we'll act like it. The truth is that we can rely on God after the fallout of our dreams. Other people and circumstances are hardly in our control. We can't force someone to say or do something when they aren't willing. We can't manipulate a situation in such a way that benefits us each and every day of our existence. We can't rewind the order of events to prevent the fallout, the breakdown, or the horrible loss. We just plain can't control the world. But we can focus on what we *can* control—our attitudes and our actions.

About ten years ago, I met Harmony, a lovely woman who has since become a cherished friend. She is the executive director of Treasures, a ministry to women in the sex industry. Harmony serves women in the industry in Los Angeles with a message of hope and truth, second chances, and grace; and she trains women all around the world to reach a population of women worthy of the love and forgiveness of Jesus. She is a world changer if I've ever met one. Not six months after I met her, she found out that her husband of several years had been having affairs.

This was a couple who met at church, engaged in premarital counseling, and set their marriage up for success. They had a blissful few years and together brought a precious little girl into the world. They had the ministry, the marriage, and the baby, but it wasn't perfect. With a confession from her husband, Harmony's world came crashing down around her. Her dreams of a wholesome family were broken.

In her own childhood, Harmony longed for the safety and security of a healthy, intact family. With a rocky upbringing tucked in her past and her life with her daughter ahead of her, Harmony had decisions to make. Like any woman facing betrayal, she needed to grieve what she had lost: a marriage, a future with the man she had committed her life to, and the happy family she had believed was her reality. Life reminded her that she couldn't control another person. She couldn't control whether her husband stayed or left. She was faced with her own powerlessness. Her husband ultimately chose to abandon his wedding vows, leaving Harmony with a broken ending to the story of their marriage.

"Is This My Life?"

As Harmony discovered, everything can change in one moment. Suddenly your life is drastically different than what it was before. It's as though your life's trajectory is reworked at lightning speed without your consent. Something unforeseen happens without your knowledge or input, or you make a decision that alters the course of your life; and the consequences, whether at your own hand or the hand of another, are severe.

Moses, chosen by God for dreams of freedom, was a man overcome by the struggles around him, and in a split second he made a decision that changed everything. At some point in Moses' story, he discovered he was of Hebrew blood. The Scriptures do not indicate how or when he found out, only that he knew. He knew that things were not as they should be. He knew a broken system surrounded him while he enjoyed privilege from his adoptive family that resembled nothing of the plight his Hebrew brothers and sisters endured.

In Exodus 2, we learn of Moses' heartache over his people and his action that changed everything:

> [11]*Many years later, when Moses had grown up, he went out to visit his own people, the Hebrews, and he saw how hard they were forced to work. During his visit, he saw an Egyptian beating one of his fellow Hebrews.* [12]*After looking in all directions to make sure no one was watching, Moses killed the Egyptian and hid the body in the sand.*
>
> [13]*The next day, when Moses went out to visit his people again, he saw two Hebrew men fighting. "Why are you beating up your friend?" Moses said to the one who had started the fight.*
>
> [14]*The man replied, "Who appointed you to be our prince and judge? Are you going to kill me as you killed that Egyptian yesterday?"*
>
> *Then Moses was afraid, thinking, "Everyone knows what I did."* [15]*And sure enough, Pharaoh heard what had happened, and he tried to kill Moses. But Moses fled from Pharaoh and went to live in the land of Midian.*
>
> *(Exodus 2:11-15)*

Before he murdered the Egyptian, I wonder if Moses intended to enjoy the Egyptian lifestyle for the rest of his life. I wonder if his life goals included settling down with an Egyptian wife and inviting her to live the high life as he knew it. His life was rerouted when he chose to murder an Egyptian and hide him in the sand. Word got back to Pharaoh of his crime, and from that point on Moses had a target on his back. His life would never be the same. He would never be welcomed back to the people or place he had called home. He would never enjoy the privilege or status he previously had received. The dream of home was broken, never to be restored to its former glory.

I can only imagine that after Moses fled Egypt, he longed and wept for home, aching for the security he once knew. Now the only life he had known was in the rearview mirror, and a new, unknown one lay before him. He must have felt a heavy sense of grief and loss as he made his way to Midian.

You and I may not have fled the country after committing a crime, knowing we would never be welcomed back, but many of us have lost our "normal" as we knew it. We've experienced broken relationships, job loss, a difficult diagnosis, or grief due to horrific events we didn't expect. Whatever happened, we lost the world we knew and were faced with the reality that things would never be the same. It's devastating to long for what used to be with no way of quickly fixing our broken hearts.

Our broken hearts, ones that are tender and bruised, are not unseen by God. He is gracious and kind in His ways toward us— able to redeem our dreams when we thought all hope was lost. He can do the impossible and repair our broken hearts as we lean into Him. He is acquainted with our grief and near to the brokenhearted. In the moments when our world falls apart, He sustains us through unthinkable experiences. Nothing is too much or too broken for the way of the Father.

These verses from Psalm 34 encourage us to turn toward the Lord in our time of need:

*⁴I prayed to the LORD, and he answered me.
    He freed me from all my fears.
⁵Those who look to him for help will be radiant with joy;
    no shadow of shame will darken their faces.
⁶In my desperation I prayed, and the LORD listened;
    he saved me from all my troubles.
⁷For the angel of the LORD is a guard;
    he surrounds and defends all who fear him.*

*⁸Taste and see that the LORD is good.
    Oh, the joys of those who take refuge in him!
⁹Fear the LORD, you his godly people,
    for those who fear him will have all they need.
¹⁰Even strong young lions sometimes go hungry,
    but those who trust in the LORD will lack no good
    thing.*

*¹⁷The LORD hears his people when they call to him for help.
    He rescues them from all their troubles.
¹⁸The LORD is close to the brokenhearted;
    he rescues those whose spirits are crushed.*

*¹⁹The righteous person faces many troubles,
    but the LORD comes to the rescue each time.*

(Psalm 34:4-10, 17-19)

Dear one, I know these words to be true! I've shared how I have found myself under a heap of broken dreams, ones I was sure would turn out peachy in just about every area of my life: the dreams of children, marriage, professional aspirations, and other relationships. But none of those dreams turned out how I thought it should. Every time things went awry I called out in desperation for the Lord to draw near, and He made Himself plain on each heart-wrenching occasion.

He has been my Rescuer and Comforter when I didn't see how what was wrong would ever be made right.

When I called on the Lord, my own heart found solace in the refuge of the King. It didn't always mean my circumstance changed, but I did. His faithfulness became my confidence. He led me to a place of healing and restoration where I could work through my fears, my unhealthy choices, and my ways of thinking that needed to be renewed. That is the God we serve. One who rescues us and does not abandon us. One who teaches us and does not scold us. One who renews us instead of punishing us. That's how our God works. That's how our Dream Giver leads us.

It's Not Over

When our dreams are crushed before our very eyes, when utter destruction flattens our hearts, it can feel impossible to think things could ever be remade. Broken dreams carry with them a heavy sense of permanence that sinks our emotional ship. When things seem really bad, hard, and impossible, we can ask ourselves, *Where do we go from here?* In the wake of broken dreams, the most honest thing we can do is seek healing for our hearts. Before we *do* anything, we must discover how to *be* the women God is longing for us to be in our season of loss.

My precious friend Harmony, whom I mentioned earlier, was committed to emotional, relational, and spiritual healing after her marriage crumbled. In an effort to heal, she drove seventy-four miles from LA to support group meetings in Orange County with a ten-month-old strapped in the back seat. She desperately wanted to find redemption from the hurt harbored deep in her heart, and she found that God was with her, redeeming her broken pieces. As she dealt with her denial, she realized her marriage had become something far different than what she planned. She identified what she wanted and needed in order to live in a healthy marriage, and she gave up trying to own others' choices, keeping them from their consequences.

As time progressed, she sensed the Lord was asking her to wait for what He had for her, to never settle for anything less than what she had come to desire. The perception of her dream was only a slice of the glory that was to come.

After her divorce was final, which took nearly three years, Harmony continued to rebuild her life. She had lost her home and her credit was ruined. With resolve and determination she made the adjustment from two incomes to one in costly Southern California. For many years Harmony made dinner for two, her daughter and herself, wishing someday she would share her table with a husband who cared for her heart and the heart of her daughter.

On her blog, Harmony wrote,

> At one point, I found myself truly grieving this and said to God, "It didn't turn out how I thought it would." I cried to God, "It wasn't supposed to turn out this way."
>
> God listened.
>
> And then, He spoke to my heart.
>
> *I rescued you.*
>
> The absurdity of this statement was almost laughable. There was nothing about what I was going through that even remotely resembled rescuing.
>
> *Harmony, I rescued you.*
>
> I was perplexed. He had my attention.
>
> *I rescued you from your version of the dream....*
>
> *I will redeem the dream.*

> This promise, that God would redeem the dream, that He
> would restore family to me carried me through. Most days,
> I held on to it. When the truth of it felt faint and distant, my
> friends would lovingly remind me of this promise . . .
> "God will redeem the dream. He will restore family to you.
> This was His promise."[1]

In the waiting that follows broken dreams, it will serve us well to keep our eyes and hearts focused on becoming women of resolve who trust the Lord. We may be tempted to settle for anything that feels comfortable or gives us a sense of security or hope, but as the Lord works in us, we can trust Him. We can trust Him with every inch of our lives and dreams. We can offer Him pliable hearts that He can redeem, avoiding the quick fix that is often too good to be true.

Temporary fixes or comforts may just push us two steps backward from what we really desire. In our effort to self-soothe we settle, and it feels like winning. It's not. Harmony says, "We are inclined to sacrifice the dream for what is temporary. The comfort our vices bring are fleeting and shallow at best, viciously destructive at worst."[2] It's true. Our trust in God and commitment to His plans, even when they feel impossible and beyond reach, stretch us to be women of hope and vision. Our dreams may have been broken, but our hearts are still beating. It's not over. As we wait well on God, we may just find that we become stronger than we thought we could be, braver than we were before, and available to witness miracles at the hand of our faithful God.

Many years later, on March 14, 2015, Harmony walked down the aisle and committed her life to a man she could have only dreamed of. A gracious, strong, and kind man who volunteered on the Treasures team—serving faithfully for women to know their value because of a loving, redeeming God—pursued Harmony. She had come to admire his character, heart, and utter devotion to the Lord. They fell for each other, and they didn't try to fix each other but committed to love each other and spur each other on in the name of love and grace. Today they have a sweet baby boy, yet another reminder of God's ability to redeem broken dreams. Harmony herself tells me that although her life took turns she never would have wanted, she wouldn't trade it for anything. God has been her King and has led her to wholeness and freedom. He has redeemed her dreams.

Sometimes God redeems our dreams without our picture-perfect wishes coming true. We hope and dream but the husband might not come. The dream job might not ever be ours. We might not ever hold that precious baby we desire so badly. Yet God redeems our dreams by ushering in a season of sweet contentment, filling us with unspeakable joy, and gifting to us His inexplicable peace.

As we process through our journeys, wondering if God sees us, hears us, and knows our hearts' desires, may we remember there are precious gifts available in the process. Who we become is as important as what we are pursuing. May we be women who can grow through the difficult seasons of life and savor the sweet seasons of life, remembering that even the good plans God has for us can seem too hard to bear if we aren't seeking Him for courage and peace. But as we seek the Lord, we can fully trust that He will redeem our dreams because it isn't over until God says so. Despite what we see and feel, despite the equity in our emotional or physical bank accounts, it's not over. Our God is working within us for our wholeness, our redemption, and our good.

Don't Let Your Broken Moments Call the Shots

I am the first to admit that my past broken moments can easily seep into my present choices without my always realizing it. Experiences that led me to a painful place, where I felt like a failure, echo into my present day. I am reminded that once upon a time things didn't go as planned, and it could easily happen again. If I don't let my past stay exactly where it belongs, which is behind me, then I can perpetuate the cycle of defeat and feel inadequate to move forward toward my God-sized dream.

When we first pursue the dream that beats in our heart, we may or may not consider everything that could go wrong. When we inevitably find ourselves in a place where things aren't exactly as we imagined they would be but, in fact, have turned into what some might describe as a dumpster fire, that is the moment when we feel that the fears we've harbored all along have come true. Fear will stop a dream dead in its tracks. Fear will tell us that we were never fit for big dreams in the first place. Fear will have us wondering if our dreams are even worth pursuing. I tell you this now, friend: fear deserves no seat at the table as you pick up the pieces of your dream. When we make decisions that affect our families, income, relationships, community, and destiny, it is imperative that we exchange fear for love.

When we move forward toward our dreams, taking the lessons we've learned from our broken moments with us, we are stronger, not weaker.

Love, we are told in the Scriptures, "never gives up, never loses faith, is always hopeful, and endures through every circumstance" (1 Corinthians 13:7). It is love, sourced by the Father Himself, that gives us the strength to endure the unthinkable and leads us to a place where we can move forward with fresh eyes and renewed hearts. Our broken moments aren't the end of the story but simply a page of the book; and when we move forward toward our dreams, taking the lessons we've learned from our broken moments with us, we are stronger, not weaker.

We are active participants in the destiny of our lives. The character we opt to display and the actions we take *after* things go wrong go a long way in seeing our dreams come alive. Our broken dreams may be life-changing, defeating, and downright awful, but God is not done with us. He doesn't leave his daughters with broken dreams. He ends the story not with brokenness but with wholeness, redemption, and resurrection.

3

Rewarding Life and Rewarding Work

3

Rewarding Life and Rewarding Work

Many moons ago as a baby-faced newlywed, I stood over the worn stove in the tiniest kitchen of our five-hundred-square-foot apartment and chipped off burned mashed potatoes from the bottom of our shiny new pots. Unbeknownst to me, at the very same time I allowed thick, chunky steaks to overcook in the oven. I was a culinary arsonist who wondered if she would ever be good at all things domestic and be able to hustle hard at my job too. I subconsciously thought I had to choose: become a domestic goddess or a boss. Little did I know, at the ripe age of twenty-two, that my internal struggle was the struggle of women across the world since the beginning of time.

In 1960, Betty Friedan, a woman who was honest with herself and the world, penned an article in *Good Housekeeping* that shook many American women of the 1960s. Let's be honest, it's still shaking some women today. The article "Women Are People, Too!" was the beginning, some say, of modern feminism. While that may be debatable and there is much controversy surrounding the term itself, I appreciate her gusto and passion in advocating for a broader vision of women's roles and opportunities.

Betty felt that women often struggled in silence with what to do with their lives. They loved their families and served their children, but some were left asking, "Is this all there is?" She believed society informed women most often about things such as "how to catch a man and keep him; how to breast-feed children and handle toilet training, sibling rivalry, adolescent rebellion; how to buy a dishwasher, cook Grandmother's bread and gourmet snails, build a swimming pool with our own hands; how to dress, look, and act more feminine, and make marriage more exciting; how to keep our husbands from dying young and our sons from growing into delinquents."[1]

Betty was discouraged with the way that society generally led women to live their lives. Girls usually were not encouraged to set their sights beyond anything but being a good wife and mother. Now, I'm *for* being a wife and mother! I'm one myself, and I love my husband and children dearly. I applaud the encouragement we find in Proverbs 31 to be a wife of noble character and a nurturing mother. But I know that each and every one of us was built for a rewarding home life *and* a rewarding work life—whatever that might look like. We don't have to choose. It isn't one over the other. We can find harmony in both. But it's important to understand what I mean by the word *work*. I'm not talking about work in the traditional 9 to 5 sense. I mean dreams of laboring over your passion—what sparks joy within you. It could be something you do for an hour a week or forty hours a week.

I tear up at the idea of sacrificing some of my dreams simply because I am married or have children. Yet for years this was the dominant narrative that women were expected to believe and live out—and in some places it still is. Even if there isn't one soul teaching us this particular way of thinking, we sometimes can come to the conclusion on our own that if we want a family, then we must give up the parts of us that dream wild dreams and the wild adventures that stir our souls. Some women sacrifice dreams for other reasons, such as caring for aging parents or other family members or meeting some pressing need that cannot be ignored. While there are seasons of life that demand our complete time and energy on the home front, it is crazy to accept that we must forfeit rewarding work altogether because a specific season invites our all. The dreams that kept us up at night when we were young (I'm talking God-shaped dreams here, not schoolgirl dreams) just might be the same ones that keep us up today.

If we wonder whether we are allowed and privileged to have both a rewarding home life and rewarding work (passions we labor over), we need only search the Scriptures to find beautiful examples of women who had both. I double-dog dare you to take a peek at Mary, the Mother of Jesus, and the revered Proverbs 31 woman as exhibits of women who slayed at this. Actually, the epilogue of Proverbs 31 is a poem or song of praise for all women, not a characterization of any one woman—with each verse beginning with a letter of the Hebrew alphabet. Even so, she represents the praiseworthy accomplishments of all women who are passionate and purposed. Both Mary and the Proverbs 31 woman affirm that we can have dreams of having a family or a personal life and rewarding work (though I'm not advocating an "I can do everything" mentality). Rather, we learn from these women that we do not have to forfeit big dreams because we have a spouse or children or aging parents or others who may depend on us in some way. We can find fulfillment in nurturing others *and* laboring over other passions. Let's take a closer look at these two examples.

Passionate and Purposed

Both Mary and the Proverbs 31 woman show us what it means to be passionate and purposed. Let's start with our girl Mary. Mary, history tells us, was raising babies and deeply concerned for the poor and downtrodden—not to mention she raised some pretty fabulous kids. Many of us are quite familiar with her eldest; you may refer to Him as your Lord and Savior. In the New Testament, we see Mary active in ministry as she traveled with Jesus' ministry team and as she participated in the early church. We know that at some point in history Mary became a single mama, because Joseph is notably absent in Jesus' adult years; yet we see in Scripture that she is still playing an integral part in her children's lives and serving in ways that matter to her.

As for Mary's younger years, it's evident our God had dreams for her that far superseded any plan a woman could make on her own. She carried our King in her womb and raised Him with all the love she had. Mary was entrusted with a home *and* a God-sized dream to steward. She was passionate and purposed.

Author Nancy DeMoss Wolgemuth says this of young Mary,

In that act of surrender, Mary offered herself to God as a living sacrifice. She was willing to be used by God for his purposes— willing to endure the loss of reputation that was certain to follow when people realized she was with child, willing to endure the ridicule and even the possible stoning permitted by the Mosaic law, willing to go through nine months of increasing discomfort and sleeplessness, willing to endure the labor pains of giving birth to the Child. Mary was willing to give up her own plans and agenda so that she might link arms with God in fulfilling his agenda.[2]

Mary had a purpose given by God that changed the course of her life forever. She would no longer live the life she had known as she stepped into partnering with God for His great and glorious plans. We see evidence of her passion in Luke 1 as she praised God for who He is and what He had done:

> [46] *"Oh, how my soul praises the Lord.*
> [47] *How my spirit rejoices in God my Savior!*
> [48] *For he took notice of his lowly servant girl,*
> *and from now on all generations will call me blessed.*
> [49] *For the Mighty One is holy,*
> *and he has done great things for me.*
> [50] *He shows mercy from generation to generation*
> *to all who fear him.*
> [51] *His mighty arm has done tremendous things!*
> *He has scattered the proud and haughty ones.*
> [52] *He has brought down princes from their thrones*
> *and exalted the humble.*
> [53] *He has filled the hungry with good things*
> *and sent the rich away with empty hands.*
> [54] *He has helped his servant Israel*
> *and remembered to be merciful.*
> [55] *For he made this promise to our ancestors,*
> *to Abraham and his children forever."*
>
> (*Luke 1:46b-55*)

Mary was passionate about and purposed for God-sized dreams. She knew the trajectory of her life was only by the hand and grace of God. God chose Mary for a great plan, and Mary wasn't perfect. I'm sure she let Thursday night's chicken burn on occasion and, like all of us, had to find a rhythm that made room for her people and her passions. When Mary said yes to the plans of God, she said yes to a rewarding life (as a homemaker) *and* to rewarding work (bearing and raising the Son of God). After Jesus Christ, she is said to be the most known figure in all of human history.

Many years before Mary, the characteristics of women were honored in Proverbs 31. This representation of a virtuous woman is described as handling her days like a champ. Today she might be labeled with the quippy hashtag: #mompreneur or #momboss. It's probably for the best that we don't attach those pop culture labels to her, though, since even a label that is intended to ooze empowerment can easily be misunderstood. Label or not, this picture of a woman is such a gift to us all as we read about her characteristics. One would never accuse her of laziness or sloth. One might wonder what day planner she was using because it is clear she isn't a gal who is just "winging it":

> ¹⁰*Who can find a virtuous and capable wife?*
>   *She is more precious than rubies.*
> ¹¹*Her husband can trust her,*
>   *and she will greatly enrich his life.*
> ¹²*She brings him good, not harm,*
>   *all the days of her life.*
> ¹³*She finds wool and flax*
>   *and busily spins it.*
> ¹⁴*She is like a merchant's ship,*
>   *bringing her food from afar.*
> ¹⁵*She gets up before dawn to prepare breakfast for her household*
>   *and plan the day's work for her servant girls.*

¹⁶*She goes to inspect a field and buys it;*
   with her earnings she plants a vineyard.
¹⁷*She is energetic and strong,*
   a hard worker.
¹⁸*She makes sure her dealings are profitable;*
   her lamp burns late into the night.
¹⁹*Her hands are busy spinning thread,*
   her fingers twisting fiber.
²⁰*She extends a helping hand to the poor*
   and opens her arms to the needy.
²¹*She has no fear of winter for her household,*
   for everyone has warm clothes.
²²*She makes her own bedspreads.*
   She dresses in fine linen and purple gowns.
²³*Her husband is well known at the city gates,*
   where he sits with the other civic leaders.
²⁴*She makes belted linen garments*
   and sashes to sell to the merchants.
²⁵*She is clothed with strength and dignity,*
   and she laughs without fear of the future.
²⁶*When she speaks, her words are wise,*
   and she gives instructions with kindness.
²⁷*She carefully watches everything in her household*
   and suffers nothing from laziness.
²⁸*Her children stand and bless her.*
   Her husband praises her:
²⁹*"There are many virtuous and capable women in the world,*
   but you surpass them all!"
³⁰*Charm is deceptive, and beauty does not last;*
   but a woman who fears the LORD will be greatly
   praised.
³¹*Reward her for all she has done.*
   Let her deeds publicly declare her praise.

(Proverbs 31:10–31)

Evidenced by two-thirds of the passage detailing the work of daily life, the Proverbs 31 woman is a classy lady who has a clear vision for her life. The last seven verses give us a peek into her heart and her relationship with her family. She is a woman of strength, honor, and respect. Her values are evident to her family and community through her actions.

Every time I read Proverbs 31, this picture of a woman who vigorously works, creates, and perfects her passion encourages my heart and mind. While I have zero plans to spin wool or plant a vineyard, I admire her guts and grace. These verses are not meant to be a measuring stick for us but a celebration of the qualities of a woman who knows who she is and what she is gifted to do. She represents someone who doesn't quit, who doesn't let the years pass her by without being a woman of virtue *and* laboring over her passions.

A number of years ago Jodi, a mentor of mine, sat across from me at her kitchen table as we sipped coffee and ate leftover Christmas Bundt cake. We chatted about the life of a writer and Bible teacher. I sheepishly admitted to her that I felt gimmicky and self-indulgent as I tried to share my writing with the world through magazine and editorial pitches (this was before I began blogging). As someone whose work depends on public consumption, it can be exhausting to put your life's story and ideas (albeit edited) out there for the world to see. In her kind and powerful voice she responded, "Tiffany, the Proverbs 31 woman knew what she had was good. Now, you may not be selling linen scarves, but your words, both written and spoken, are good. Never apologize for sharing them with the world." I was never the same after Jodi's encouragement. She spoke those words into my heart years before I ever had a piece of work published, but it changed my outlook in an instant.

I spent the next several years tapping the keys on my keyboard with words of encouragement, honesty, and all the truth I could muster. I knew there were women—at least a handful—on the other end of my thoughts, reading the narratives of hope and courage I shared. Ten years and a couple of books and Bible studies later, I carry the same conviction I carried then. My words matter. This is my gift to the world. I am committed to a work that sparks joy within my own heart and, if all goes as planned, in the hearts of those who read it. I'll be honest, it is not easy but I wouldn't have it any other way. Most days, after wrestling with my wild little boys, I sneak up to my office to write. I hear all kinds of sounds around the corner—rattle, clank, bang, bong—coming from the living room as they do as little boys do; but I've learned to fight the urge to check on them. Their dad is fully capable of handling their chaos. My passion and purpose demand time and attention—something my heart cannot afford to pass up.

I would be lying if I said I got here on my own. My husband has been the greatest supporter of my dreams. He takes the lead on weekends so I can write and speak, and he shares the day-to-day labor to make our home run as smoothly as possible. He pushes me to invest in my gift at all costs. He is my biggest cheerleader, and we have learned to delight in serving each other. He is a big proponent of ditching any titles or assumed roles in our marriage. Together we decide who is capable of handling the issues at hand. I love him for it. As I have pursued my God-sized dream, it has taken a fair amount of reflection on what does and does not work in our home to provide the support we both need to see our dreams come to pass. My life's work and family life are intended to complement each other, combining to make one holistic, sacred life of love and passion.

Instead of viewing our home lives and passion projects as separate entities—or, dare I say, enemies—perhaps we can allow them to work together as partners to build a life we love. One mustn't come at the expense of the other. In fact, one supports the other—even enables the other to thrive. When we love our work (whatever that looks like), we often are more fulfilled in our daily activities. And when we are deeply connected to the people who make up our tribe and develop a rhythm in our home, we usually have more energy to pursue the passions that are core to who we are.

Our tribe, those we spend our life with, plays a unique role in supporting us as we pursue our dreams and play to our strengths. As I mentioned earlier, I dabbled in arson as I burned both mashed potatoes and hearty steaks to a crisp simultaneously (I'm a gifted girl). Since that season of my life, my husband, Derek, discovered he absolutely loves to cook. (I might have played a small role in that with my burned goods.) He feels at home in the kitchen, takes the lead on dinner nearly every night, and often spends his weekends baking with our kids. Many of my girlfriends spend their afternoons and evenings chopping, roasting, and braising. I don't, and that's okay. Early in our marriage, Derek and I assessed who is suited to various tasks, and we have stuck to them. We've done our absolute best to develop a rhythm in which everyone can thrive. With this rythmn we've made room for each other's strengths and room to pursue our passions.

---

*As we dream God-sized dreams,
let's refuse to be boxed in by labels or
cultural norms that do not encourage
us to be who God created us to be.*

As we dream God-sized dreams, let's refuse to be boxed in by labels or cultural norms that do not encourage us to be who God created us to be. Let's go ahead and throw all of that out for the joy of walking in our gifts, responsibilities, and skills. May we be inspired by Mary, the mother of Jesus, the Proverbs 31 woman, and the woman we've watched either from a distance or up close who loves others, including her family, and pursues her passion. You and I may never be described as perfect while we nurture others and labor over what we love, but I pray we will be described as women of conviction— pursuing our passions with grit and grace as we care for those we love, remaining attentive to their needs and rhythms. Because, dear friend, you are built for a rewarding home life *and* a rewarding work life. And that requires strength and courage.

Step Up with Strength and Courage

I remember the first time I was informed that I was direct. Yep. I was not surprised in the slightest. I wasn't labeled as bossy but direct. Dare I say, I wanted to take it as a compliment, but the giver of said comment did not mean it that way. The team with whom I worked five days a week chuckled at the comment, as did I. You see, my personality and communication style most certainly can be summed up with the words "straight shooter." I will communicate what I see with love and grace, but I won't sit silently and be agreeable for the sake of being liked or blending in unless we are deciding between choices of restaurants. Then it's dealer's choice. But what I've found is that a woman can be both direct and gentle. Life doesn't require one or the other but both together. Yet we can struggle with this.

In an effort not to be seen as intimidating, domineering, or authoritative, we sometimes choose to blend in rather than stand out.

At times we can feel we must hide our gifts when, in reality, the world needs our leadership, compassion, and voices as women.

A dear friend and I once chatted about this very issue. Both of us held positions in leadership that required decision-making, people management, and responsibility for others. While it would have been nice to be the most agreeable person in the room, in order to serve those around us best we had to make hard decisions, initiate tough conversations, and care for the souls of those we led. We had no plans to be seen as intimidating, domineering, or authoritative. Yet those of us who go against the proverbial grain by raising our wise and direct voices can be dismissed as bossy or angry or on a power trip. There are many traits that we are labeled with when we rise to pursue our dreams. Some of them are applauded and others...well...not so much.

Sometimes we are labeled as icy if we don't show "enough" emotion, but on the flipside we are labeled as fragile if we are too emotional—and can be seen as unfit to lead. Some of us have been told that we must be tough if we want to pursue our dreams in a male-dominated world and that any sign of weakness disqualifies us from our position. A woman who rises to take her place and do what God has called her to do will face judgment in some way whether she anticipates it or not.

---

*The stories of our lives are intended
to be beautiful, complete with adventure
and a fierce pursuit of what we love,
and this requires an enormous
amount of strength and courage.*

While sometimes it may be intimidating to pursue what we love, the Lord wired us for glorious plans that He planned long ago. Ephesians 2:10 tell us, "For we are God's masterpiece. He has created us anew in Christ Jesus, so we can do the good things he planned for us long ago." As we pursue our dreams, the Lord is working within us, refining us and drawing us closer to Him. The stories of our lives are intended to be beautiful, complete with adventure and a fierce pursuit of what we love, and this requires an enormous amount of strength and courage.

Very few women have had such widespread fame as that of the Iron Lady, Margaret Thatcher.[3] The term "iron lady" means "strong-willed woman" and often is used to refer to women leaders of government around the world.[4] After marrying Denis Thatcher in 1951 and welcoming her twins in 1953, Margaret spent her time training as a lawyer. Nearly twenty years later she made a splash in British politics, and everyone in the United Kingdom took notice of the rising star. She was making history and rising to the top. By this point she was well known and had yet to be appointed as prime minister.

I can only imagine the comments and stereotypes she dealt with in the 1950s, 1960s, and 1970s as a woman with a passion to lead, work, and serve those around her. That didn't stop the tenacious Margaret from doing what she thought was right to serve the people of her country. It didn't stop her from dreaming impossible dreams. When her party won the General Election in May 1979, the next day she was appointed Prime Minister of the United Kingdom of Great Britain and Northern Ireland; and she went on to serve her country as prime minister for eleven years.

Margaret, a devout follower of Jesus, was known as harsh, controversial, and even uncaring. People had their opinions of her, but that in no way stopped her from serving at the post she had been given. At times she may not have been liked, but she was leading and serving by her convictions and values; and she never backed down. Ever. After Winston Churchill, she is the most famous British politician to ever lead the country. When she died in 2013, honor was given to her by every political party. Her legacy is known throughout Britain and around the world. She was most certainly a woman who rose to the occasion, pursued her dreams, and didn't give up despite the stereotypes perpetuated by those around her.

Since the 1950s, women have risen to places of power, influence, and leadership in unprecedented ways—especially in the West. While their stories aren't necessarily the dominant narrative of our history books, there have been women who have stepped up with strong voices, convictions, and God-sized dreams. They have paved the way for so many of us to pursue our dreams in ways we may never fully understand. In the same way that the women who have gone before us have made an impact, you and I are writing history this very day. Our choices to love, serve, shepherd, lead, and pursue our passions are shaping the people around us and the culture we live in while exposing the majesty of God.

In both big and small ways, we can make a difference. You and I may not run for the highest office of the land, but we can pursue our passions in our own unique ways. My dear friend Mary sports a dress every single day of December to raise awareness and collect donations for anti–sex trafficking initiatives across the world. This past year she and her seven-year-old son went one step further and stitched bow ties for every man willing to donate more than $100. In addition to bow ties, she hosted a Dressember walk in which people walked five kilometers (with women and girls wearing dresses) to raise their own support for women trapped in sex trafficking. Mary and her son were among the top six advocates for the Dressember

Initiative. Her passion, purpose, and people convened to pursue the dream of freedom for enslaved women. Like Margaret and Mary, we can chase after our dreams and invite our families to come along; and our passions can be unleashed.

You and I weren't created to sit in silence, smile, and look pretty. We have a life to live. A life to love. We have passions to pursue, people to serve, *and* loved ones to shepherd. It will be worth it to develop our gifts and skills, raise our voices, and step up to do the very things our hearts ache to do. As the younger generations watch, may they see us as women who don't hold back because of how we may be perceived. May they see in us women who chase after the heart of God, love with compassion, and pursue our dreams with strength and courage.

4

Tell Me Why

4

Tell Me Why

One time about a dozen years ago I was on a flight from Manchester, England, to Seattle, Washington, and I sat by two women who were flying together on a business trip. After a few hours into our nine-hour flight, I made some silly comments about the airline-issued peanuts, and eventually we moved past chatting about in-flight snacks to sharing a bit about ourselves. Both of my seatmates invented scents for perfume companies. The strangers-turned-acquaintances shared about their days spent smelling various combinations of gardenia, jasmine, and peonies whipped together for delicious scents. I couldn't help wondering how they had gotten into such a unique business. They went on to share how they landed the jobs they loved, and I left my flight inspired to keep my love for what I do at the center of why I do it.

In most any conversation with a stranger, you make pleasantries so as not to look like you possess zero social skills. The most common question you and I ask of a stranger is *what* he or she does for a living. The question, "What do you do?" is easily answered by sharing what indeed you actually do. It's an easy answer for most of us. Perhaps you may say "I am a chef" or "a business analyst" or "I sell sketches of celebrities on Etsy" or "I am a full-time mom." Whatever it may be, you share what you do. If you pique the interest of your listener, you then may be asked *how* you do it. Most of us can quickly and easily share what we do and how we do it, but not all of us can share *why* we do it. Why do we tap away on our keyboards at all hours of the night? Why do we show up at our office each morning at 8:00 a.m. sharp? Why do we go to school to further our education in a particular field? Why do we give our all to running a home? Why?

Start with Why

I've found that if we can dream from the inside out, starting with why we do what we do, our values will be clear as we navigate the course of our dreams. What we do and how we do it are important, but nothing will drive us more than understanding *why* we do it. In the thick of it, too many of us throw up our hands and say, "Why am I working so hard on this?" or "Does any of this matter?" or "I'm out of my league." These are questions that expose our frustration—not with what or how we do things but with why we do those things that we dream to do. We are able to answer our own doubts and fears and handle unforeseen changes in our lives with grace if we know why we long for our dreams to come to pass.

Quite a few years ago, Jodi, my dear friend I shared about earlier, pushed me to create a mission statement for my life. At the time, I had been married only a couple of years and didn't have any kids yet, but I had a good idea of what I wanted to do. Jodi emphatically encouraged me to clearly state why I wanted to write. It wasn't enough to have talent and skill, a natural gift, or connections; she made it crystal clear that all the talent in the world wouldn't matter if you didn't know why you longed for your God-sized dream to become your reality.

Jodi shared with me her own personal mission statement, one that stood the test of time and kept her focused when different opportunities came knocking on her door. She explained that the reason it was important to know the "why" of what I was doing was to clearly communicate to my own heart its mission.

This dear mentor knew what she was talking about. Jodi married the love of her life while she was still a teenager, had three precious babies with her preacher-husband, and managed their home in her twenties. In her thirties, she began leading the women's ministry at the church where her husband pastored, as well as unofficially leading in various other capacities. She spent her days planning Bible studies for women and many late nights writing pieces to pitch to magazines and periodicals.

One year in her forties, Jodi's youngest daughter graduated high school, and that very same year she was asked to throw her name in the ring to serve as the Pacific Northwest Women's Ministry Director of her denomination, serving the women of 350 area churches. Caught off guard by the offer, her first response was no. But after prayer and fasting, she asked herself, "What if God put me on earth, at this time, to do this? To lead these women? What if this is my mission in this season of life?" As she warmed up to the idea and was eventually chosen to lead, she found herself underprepared and out of her league. Although she felt out of her element, she knew without a shadow of a doubt that she was in the will of God; her "why" was clear, demolishing any sense of inadequacy or fear. She was the girl for the job because she longed to live and love in a way that consistently compelled others to become Christ followers.

In her fifties, Jodi chose to go back to school. The girl who never finished college went back to a life of textbooks and writing assignments. The opportunity to be in school felt daunting, considering she was still working; but to live her dream in this season of life meant she would embrace lifelong learning. In seminary, she sharpened the tools God had given her and learned from different thinkers and dreamers she never would have met otherwise. She received her masters and doctorate degrees in leadership studies after six years of school.

Jodi confessed to me that certain doors never would have opened unless she had gone back to school. Opportunities to speak at university commencements, write for *The Seattle Times*, and teach as an adjunct professor were results of going back to school. In the hard moments and demanding days, her *why* kept her focused. In turn, what she did and how she did it surpassed her wildest dreams.

Without question, Jodi exists to glorify God, live a vibrant life, and chase after God-sized dreams in every season of life. She informed me that the clear path to clarifying why you want to pursue your God-sized dream is to know in your heart of hearts what you value, because our dreams are a reflection of what we value.

It's our values—the beliefs and commitments we hold dear—that will help us zero in on why we are chasing the dream, why we are waking up early to create and formulate that which is yet to be. It's our *why* that will keep us focused when our doubts and fears come creeping in—keep us from giving up on the dreams that beat loudly in our hearts. It would be a shame for us to coast on autopilot through our beautiful lives and wonder at the end why we did what we did. Our journeys are far too precious to let life pass by without knowing why we long for our dreams to become reality.

For me in this season of life, I'm more assured of why I do what I do than ever before. As I follow my beloved Jesus, love my precious family, and fearlessly make known the mysteries of the gospel to the women in my community and world with my spoken and written words as well as actions that push myself and those around me to be peacemakers and truth-tellers—I'm convinced more than ever that I was destined to do this very thing, because I'm most alive when I'm loving Christ and serving the cherished souls around me. I wouldn't want to do anything else. Having said that, my values provide me with clear direction on what to say no to. I can say no to several good opportunities in order to leave room for the great ones. I'm spending my life on opportunities that clearly align with my values and my *why*.

Life will always present us with great things to do and wonderful ways to do it, but unless something makes us come alive and is in sync with our why, *it's often best to pass.*

Life will always present us with great things to do and wonderful ways to do it, but unless something makes us come alive and is in sync with our *why*, it's often best to pass. You and I only get one chance to live this life; may we not run ourselves ragged doing every wonderful thing or something that drains us dry but, instead, do the very thing that refreshes us and draws us closer to the Father.

What about you? What makes you come alive? Why do you do what you do? What compels you to do it? What joy or blessing do you find in your dreams? Why does it matter to you if the dream becomes your reality? Knowing your *why* is critical to the life of your dreams, because without it you may be tempted to give up or give in when the going gets tough.

Friend, you were born with skills, gifts, and abilities—all perfectly unique to the woman who you are. What you do and how you do it (the method, if you will) will always be secondary to the *why*—the message you are telling your own heart and the world. Your *why* speaks loud and clear about what you value most. As you are honest with yourself and dreaming of greater things, may you always know why your dream matters, because you were born to dream.

Just Start Somewhere

After years in full-time church ministry, I stepped away to stay home with my kids, pursue writing, and begin a new chapter of my life. To end my season of church ministry was to start a new season, one that my husband and I were grossly underprepared for. Resigning from my position meant losing two-thirds of our monthly family income. At the time, my husband was an elementary school teacher, and he chose to end his career in teaching to pursue something else that would have the potential to make enough income to cover our expenses and allow me to stay home with our children and pursue my passions. It all seemed so possible—until the bills came in the mail one after another. What seemed so exciting at first quickly became one of the greatest challenges we had ever faced together. We both had worked in our respective fields for nearly ten years, and we knew starting a new chapter would be difficult—but not nearly as difficult as it turned out to be.

As I pitched essays to magazines and crafted my book proposal, my husband discovered a love for real estate. He thoroughly enjoyed the process of hunting for our home and couldn't shake the idea of helping others with one of the biggest purchases of their lives. After a couple of months of studying and becoming a licensed agent, he hit the ground running, doing his absolute best to drum up business. With a few connections to buyers and sellers, he worked his tail off to serve the few clients he had. In the early days, he called everyone he knew, even folks he knew from ten years ago, to share his new venture and serve them any way he could. He didn't know everything about the housing market and had very little to start with, but he started nonetheless.

Our mentors told us that it can be a slow start in real estate and many agents quit after about eighteen months. We found out why. Although we had saved up about seven months' worth of income, it didn't last. In his first year in real estate, he made less than $10,000. No lie. It was a slow start. As I watched him start over in a new career, I witnessed a man who trusted God with his whole heart humbly go after his dream. No matter who we are, the pursuit of our dreams invites us to learn new ways of doing things and sharpens our God-given skills while trusting the Lord with everything that's precious to us. It's a ton of work. It's emotional, mental, and even physical work to start something new.

Our new chapter, one we had been so eager to begin, was peppered with tearful prayers. We questioned each other and wondered if we had made the right decision. Yet we couldn't deny that God was calling us to something new, something great, something we couldn't walk away from. Although the conditions were far from ideal—with mouths to feed, a monthly mortgage payment due on our house that we had purchased a year before, and little resources to begin with— we started.

It can be overwhelming to think of how to start doing the very thing we wish to do. Yet we must start somewhere. God-sized dreams demand participation on our part. It's too easy to let months or years pass without taking the first step. But once we take the first step, we can march, shimmy, or hustle in the direction of our dreams. One two-step at a time. If we begin with the end in mind, we can remember that the pursuit is a process—one that is exciting and exhausting, costly and consuming.

You see, no one is an expert at the beginning of anything. No one is an expert skier or master photographer out of the gate. We don't start on the black diamond ski run or convince someone to let us photograph her wedding when we haven't done our due diligence and clocked the time to become an expert. Life doesn't work like that. We all have to start somewhere. We all have to begin, learn the ropes, and go after it. I get it; we want to be instantly awesome at whatever it is that burns inside our hearts. If we aren't instantly a grand master genius at whatever our heart dreams of, we may forgo the dream altogether, assuming that if we don't experience instant success, then God isn't in it. Yet in starting we are stretched and invited to trust the Lord and humbly learn, listen, and try our hand at whatever we are eager to do.

Conditions will never be absolutely perfect to pursue our dreams. We tell ourselves, "When life slows down or when I have this or that, then I will get after it, but not until then." What if life doesn't slow down? What if there is never a perfect time to start? What if the rocky season or the busy season or the chaotic season is the very season you should start pursuing your God-sized dream? What if the time is now? What if the Lord is completely fine that you don't know it all? What if He is totally cool with your trusting Him for the victory as you chase after the dream? What if that was part of His plan all along?

I doubt Noah or Moses or Nehemiah felt that they were in an ideal season to start something and go after what God had called them to do. Yet they did it. They started with big hearts and even bigger obstacles, and they trusted their faithful God. We can do the same. When we start pursuing the God-sized dreams in our hearts, like the saints of old, we begin with faith, facing the fears and obstacles with trust. God's faithfulness is our confidence to overcome obstacles, learn through our mistakes, and do what He set in our hearts to do. We see this so clearly in Moses' story.

Midian

After he fled Egypt, Moses landed in Midian; and although he may not have realized it, God was preparing Moses for plans that he would never feel fully ready to execute. Yet God worked in His mysterious, right-on-time ways.

Exodus 2:15-25 tells us what happened in Midian:

> *15And sure enough, Pharaoh heard what had happened, and he tried to kill Moses. But Moses fled from Pharaoh and went to live in the land of Midian.*
>
> *When Moses arrived in Midian, he sat down beside a well. 16Now the priest of Midian had seven daughters who came as usual to draw water and fill the water troughs for their father's flocks. 17But some other shepherds came and chased them away. So Moses jumped up and rescued the girls from the shepherds. Then he drew water for their flocks.*
>
> *18When the girls returned to Reuel, their father, he asked, "Why are you back so soon today?"*
>
> *19"An Egyptian rescued us from the shepherds," they answered. "And then he drew water for us and watered our flocks."*

> ²⁰*"Then where is he?" their father asked. "Why did you leave him there? Invite him to come and eat with us."*
>
> ²¹*Moses accepted the invitation, and he settled there with him. In time, Reuel gave Moses his daughter Zipporah to be his wife.* ²²*Later she gave birth to a son, and Moses named him Gershom, for he explained, "I have been a foreigner in a foreign land."*
>
> ²³*Years passed, and the king of Egypt died. But the Israelites continued to groan under their burden of slavery. They cried out for help, and their cry rose up to God.* ²⁴*God heard their groaning, and he remembered his covenant promise to Abraham, Isaac, and Jacob.* ²⁵*He looked down on the people of Israel and knew it was time to act.*

Tucked in this portion of Scripture we find a glimpse, a foreshadowing, of the man Moses would become. His heroic leadership would one day lead the Israelites to freedom, but for now he was an aid to a few women who were bullied by shepherds. As the women returned home, their father was surprised they were back so soon. Some commentators have determined his shock to his daughters' early return was due to daily bullying by the shepherds, who refused to allow their sheep to drink from the trough.[1] That is, until Moses came onto the scene.

Moses had within him a heart for justice, strong conviction, and courage to defend the powerless women. Previously, Moses had killed a man when he witnessed injustice, but we read of no force or violence on the part of Moses this time. Somehow—either by persuasive words or perhaps because he, dressed in fine Egyptian clothing, appeared to be a man of power—Moses managed to defend the women, allowing them to do what they had gathered at the well to do.

Like Moses, we have convictions that supersede our fears. Moses may have feared the shepherds, but his conviction to defend the women was greater than his fear of man. What was within him was greater than what was outside of him. He knew *why* he had to defend them. He couldn't stand by when he had in his power the ability to help them.

Later in the passage we discover that Moses married one of Reuel's daughters and had a son with her. He had a new normal that was far different than his earlier years in Egypt. A new season brought new opportunity, love, and family. It's likely that Moses never would have chosen life in Midian if fear for his own life had not led him there. Like Moses, our lives can sometimes feel completely out of our control. We exit from a season or relationship only to be met by new challenges in the next one. New opportunities and relationships bring with them their own new struggles, but God is with us every step of the way. He is not absent.

Although we don't witness God's audible voice written into the story of Moses' life just yet, He was there from the very beginning. He was not surprised or perplexed by the plot twist. The last three verses of Exodus 2 inform us that back in Egypt, the king had died and the Israelites were still serving as slaves to their masters in captivity. They continued to groan under their burden of bondage, but God heard their cries. It was time to act. Yet we see that Moses had some reservations. Call it insecurity, self-doubt, or anxiety; but pure and simple, it was debilitating fear. We've all been there.

I Can't, Though

Take it from a girl who once hid in the bathroom and puked at work because of anxiety. I get it. I do. You have a plan, a rough estimation of how things will work out if you pursue your dreams, but you find yourself debilitated by fear. You just can't start. You've placed your dreams on the top shelf, letting them collect dust, and you've continued to do what you've always done. I feel you; the familiar is comforting. But in your heart of hearts you were built to dream, to partner with God for His glory, to create, to design, to do things that take work and effort; and you most certainly have to start somewhere.

Our man Moses, who was invited by the Divine to lead the Israelites to freedom, was quick to remind God that maybe he wasn't the guy for the job. God's impossible plans were probably not in Moses' five-year plan, but God's power was available to Moses. And His timing was perfect.

In Exodus 3, we find Moses intrigued by a burning bush that didn't actually burn up. Better yet, he was more than intrigued, maybe even terrified, once the voice of God spoke through said bush. He knew this was far from normal when the God of heaven and earth informed him to take off his sandals. In the ancient east, sandals normally would be removed in a place of worship or at the home of an honored person. The presence of God most certainly qualifies as both. Exodus 3:7-15 tells us what happened next:

> [7]Then the LORD told him, "I have certainly seen the oppression of my people in Egypt. I have heard their cries of distress because of their harsh slave drivers. Yes, I am aware of their suffering. [8]So I have come down to rescue them from the power of the Egyptians and lead them out of Egypt into their own fertile and spacious land. It is a land flowing with milk and honey—the land where the Canaanites, Hittites, Amorites, Perizzites, Hivites, and Jebusites now live. [9]Look! The cry of the people of Israel has reached me, and I have seen how harshly the Egyptians abuse them. [10]Now go, for I

am sending you to Pharaoh. You must lead my people Israel
out of Egypt."

¹¹But Moses protested to God, "Who am I to appear before
Pharaoh? Who am I to lead the people of Israel out of
Egypt?"

¹²God answered, "I will be with you. And this is your
sign that I am the one who has sent you: When you have
brought the people out of Egypt, you will worship God at
this very mountain."

¹³But Moses protested, "If I go to the people of Israel and
tell them, 'The God of your ancestors has sent me to you,'
they will ask me, 'What is his name?' Then what should I
tell them?"

¹⁴God replied to Moses, "I AM WHO I AM. Say this to the
people of Israel: I AM has sent me to you." ¹⁵God also said
to Moses, "Say this to the people of Israel: Yahweh, the God
of your ancestors—the God of Abraham, the God of Isaac,
and the God of Jacob—has sent me to you.

This is my eternal name,
    my name to remember for all generations.

First of all, if we read Exodus 3:1, we see that Moses is tending
the sheep of his father-in-law, Jethro, while in Exodus 2:18 his father-
in-law is called Ruel. What's up with that? Some scholars suggest that
Reuel is simply another name for Jethro, much like Jacob is also called
Israel. Others say that Jethro might have been his priestly name. In
any case, most believe this is one and the same man.

So, Moses had his marching orders from Father God, and they
were no joke. They were plans that would change the course of an

entire people group for generations to come. Now, if you'll recall, Moses' work experience for this monumental job included murder of an Egyptian man, the rescue of his father-in-law's daughters, and sheep herding. Yet the mighty call of God on his life superseded his track record or prior work experience. In fact, Moses' life up to that point served as his preparation for leading the Israelites. He was born to dream and partner with God for the impossible, just like you and me.

As you consider all God has called you to do, ask yourself, *What if I don't start?* What if I don't chase the dream that burns within my heart? What if I give up right out of the gate? What will my life look like? What will I miss out on? Can my heart afford to defer my dreams? Will I allow my fears to drive my actions or inactions? Do they dictate the inner workings of my thoughts?

When we start pursuing the dreams in our hearts, we are often provided with ample opportunity to face our fears. When we start, with our limited knowledge but willing hearts, we are acutely aware of what we don't know and what we don't have. The fear of humiliation or of what we'll lose is too much to take. We know others who've tried and failed, and we allow the hard moments in their journeys to impact ours in a way that was never meant to be. We convince ourselves that it would be irresponsible to pursue what beats loudly in our chests. In reality, we let our fears rule the roost. I am aware there are times when we should wait on pursuing our dreams and we'll discuss that more later, but that's not what I'm talking about here. I'm referring to the times that the Lord said, *"Go!"* and you and I said, *"No!"*

When fear keeps us from starting, convincing us that it won't work out or that we aren't gifted or skilled enough to dream God-sized dreams, it's helpful to play it out. What will it look like if our worst fears happen? What will it look like if our best attempts fail miserably?

Could it be that the Lord will be with us, guiding us through victory and defeat, through the ups and the downs? Could it be that He is ready and willing to lend strength and grow our character and capacity through our journeys? I believe so. Our God is faithful to lead us, support us, and fight for us. He is greater, much greater, than the worst fears we can imagine. We can start pursuing the God-sized dreams, face our fears with Him, and discover the depth of His grace and companionship as we do.

Whatever it is God has called us to do, we'll discover the kind character and companionship of the Father in a new way as we start. In fact, from the minute we start, no matter what the circumstance may be, He is with us. May we remember with whom we are partnering. He is the God of Abraham, Isaac, and Jacob. He is the God of Moses and Joshua, of Nehemiah and Noah. He is the God of Joan of Arc and Harriet Tubman, of Dr. Martin Luther King Jr. and Billy Graham. He is the God who loves us, sent His Son to die for us, and will be with us for all of our days. With Him we can start pursuing our dreams, and on Him we can rely for victory!

5

Haters Gonna Hate

5

Haters Gonna Hate

About a year ago, I listened to an author share a horrifying story of how her book was torn up and sent to her in the mail. I couldn't imagine opening a package to find my work ripped to shreds and intentionally sent to my home to hurt me. Yet this strong woman humbly shared her story to a hushed crowd. Thousands revere this author, but she is, in fact, a human being with emotions and feelings; and a single act of hate can feel like two to the chest. It's easy to allow one comment, one antagonistic act from another, to drown out the accomplishment or acclaim we've received.

We are warned not to share our hopes and dreams in their infancy with just anyone—and for good reason. Someone else's critical response to our dreams can leave us feeling defeated and cause us to question if God is leading us or if our dream is even worth pursuing. Even worse, when the dream takes root in reality, it can be heart-wrenching to witness another hate on what God is birthing, doing, or achieving within us. Haters will always be around, but they must never dampen our days.

The great Maya Angelou in her poem "Haters" teaches us, "The problem I have with haters is that they see my glory, but they don't know my story."[1] I imagine Maya's words of instruction in this poem are from a place of experience. She was a dreamer, not unlike you and me, who faced opposition. She was a woman of conviction who encouraged all of us to raise our voices and pursue freedom. Yet for all the good she stood for, she experienced haters, ones who looked to knock her down a few pegs on her journey. In her poem, Maya gives us wise advice on how to handle the haters: don't let the haters get a foothold in our hearts, and point them to the Lord for all He has done. Thank you, Maya.

Let's unpack that wise advice together.

Shade, Shade, Shade

When you find yourself on the receiving end of someone else's disdain for your work in the pursuit of your dream, first listen. Do your best to discover where they are coming from. Were you misunderstood? Were you accused of something you didn't do? Do they disagree with what you stand for or what you've done, and are they doing everything in their power to ensure that you are aware of it? What is it that caused them to "go off" in the first place? When we understand where folks are coming from we can dismantle the offense. I'm not saying it won't be painful to be "hated on," but I am saying it gives us a next step in a tender moment. We can call it for what it is when we understand where folks are coming from.

Once we identify how someone has made us feel for what God is doing in our lives, we have options. Now, I understand that in the heat of the moment, you may want to exchange choice words with the scoffer of your life and work, but in the words of the fictional princess,

Elsa, *"Let it goooo."* Your heart has no business entertaining hatred for what God is doing in you, because as you identify who you are in Christ, there is no room for guilt and shame from another. No room to feel insignificant because someone else is jealous or delights in feeling tall when he or she makes you feel small. This is much harder said than done. It can knock you off your feet when someone spits a cruel word your way, but you are not defined by other people's opinions. A holy God who loves you defines you. As the haters do their thing, let it be an opportunity to celebrate what God is doing within you. The Divine is orchestrating your days, not your haters. A Giver of dreams, hopes, truth, and courage leads you.

A few years ago I wrote a piece titled "My Son Doesn't Know He's Black" for a popular mommy blog. My son was adopted at two-and-a-half years old from Uganda. In the essay, I explained that my son wasn't familiar with what it means to be black in America. When I wrote the piece he was barely four years old and had zero knowledge of the slave trade, Jim Crow, the Emancipation Proclamation, Bloody Sunday, the march on Washington, or the civil rights movement. He didn't understand the significance of what was happening in places like Ferguson, McKinney, Cleveland, or Sanford. I went on to explain that there would soon come a day when he would discover the remarkable efforts of Frederick Douglass, Dr. Martin Luther King Jr., Rosa Parks, John Lewis, Jackie Robinson, John Perkins, Bryan Stevenson, and hundreds upon hundreds of others who fought, and continue to fight, for equal rights. In time, he would learn of the pain, grief, and injustice African Americans have endured in this country and also how they've brought light and freedom to our country. I ended my piece by explaining that as his mama, I would teach him to be a man of respect, honor, and love and to treat others with kindness no matter the color of another's skin. After it was posted, guess what happened? People lost their minds. I received a fair amount of love and a hefty amount of shade. Women, with strong words, accused me of poisoning my child's mind, and many claimed that they would never allow their children to see color.

In the responses to the article there were several assumptions made about me, my family, and the way I raise my children. I was shocked for about .003 seconds that someone would disagree with my message, but I learned quickly that everyone has an opinion and, more often than not, feels the need to share what he or she thinks regardless of how it would make another feel.

If God is on the move in your life
and you keep in step with Him,
you can silence the discouragement
from those you thought
would root you on.

If someone disagrees with what we stand for, what we are doing, or what we've accomplished, we do not, under any circumstance, have to allow him or her to have a voice in our lives. You may agree with me but wonder, "What if that person is close to me? What if that person is someone who has been in my life for ages but now chooses to oppose or demean my God-sized dream?" Life gets tricky when someone you care for is threatened by or jealous of what God is working through you. However, if God is on the move in your life and you keep in step with Him, you can silence the discouragement from those you thought would root you on.

Moses, Nehemiah, David, Jeremiah, Jesus, the adulterous woman, Paul, and dozens of others dealt with haters in their time—at a distance and up close. They were met with opposition, lies, gossip, and mockery for the purposes and plans God had for each of them. It would be silly to think we could float through this life without someone else opposing what God is doing within us. As Maya said, "They see my glory, but they don't know my story." Not everyone will be rooting us on in this life. They won't see the whole picture or understand the whole plan, and it isn't for them anyway. Our purposes and plans instilled in us by our gracious God don't require the approval of those who don't respect us.

Haters cause us to ask the question, "Why don't you like me? What's your problem with me?" Their actions pinch a nerve that proves painful—so painful at times that we can't get our minds off of it. As we question ourselves, let us go to the throne of God and be reminded that we are loved. We are enough. We are gifted. We are called. We are purposed. A holy God leads us. We are built for the glory of God. We are living our story, one full of highs and lows, sacrifices and gains. Like Moses, may we be dreamers who will not stop for those who hate. Never. Ever. Even if they cause us to question God.

When Haters Cause Us to Doubt

After his encounter with God at the burning bush in Midian, Moses said yes to the plans of God and willingly packed up his family to journey toward Egypt, carrying the staff of God with him. With the blessing of his father-in-law, he set out against the odds to do what God had for him to do. Moses was called by God to lead His people to freedom, but he had haters—and not just any haters. Moses had haters who possessed great power to demean and abuse the Israelites.

Pharaoh, whose heart was hardened by God Himself (Exodus 4:21), not only challenged Moses but also made God's beloved people suffer for Moses' request. Moses requested of Pharaoh a brief recess to hold a festival in the wilderness to honor God. Pharaoh replied with a solid no by forcing the Israelites to work harder, with fewer building materials, and still produce the same quota of bricks they had previously been assigned to make. Not only was Moses' request denied; the Israelite foremen were fuming mad:

> [19] *The Israelite foremen could see that they were in serious trouble when they were told, "You must not reduce the number of bricks you make each day."* [20] *As they left Pharaoh's court, they confronted Moses and Aaron, who were waiting outside for them.* [21] *The foremen said to them, "May the LORD judge and punish you for making us stink before Pharaoh and his officials. You have put a sword into their hands, an excuse to kill us!"*
>
> [22] *Then Moses went back to the LORD and protested, "Why have you brought all this trouble on your own people, Lord? Why did you send me?* [23] *Ever since I came to Pharaoh as your spokesman, he has been even more brutal to your people. And you have done nothing to rescue them!"*
>
> (*Exodus 5:19-23*)

Pharaoh, in his power, made the lives of the Israelites absolutely miserable. As Moses stood for justice and freedom, Pharaoh's actions led to severe physical abuse of the people of God. Not only did Pharaoh reject Moses' plea to free the people of God; his actions led Moses to question the Lord in verse 22, wondering why the Lord would bring this tragedy upon His people and why He had done nothing to rescue them. If they get under our skin, our haters, like Pharaoh, can make us question the kindness, sovereignty, and plans of God.

Haters, you see, come in all shapes and sizes. They can be passive-aggressive toward you and the dreams you pursue, or they can come at you full force with hurtful words and actions that undercut all you believe God is doing within you and through you. In those moments, may we cry out to the Father as Moses did so that He can help us to protect our minds, gird our resolve, and claim the truth of God's word and promises.

Dear Friends

After crying out to our God, we can then find additional support from dear friends.

A dear friend of mine with her own dreams, haters, challenges, and ups and downs has been a safe place to me for quite some time. We've nurtured our friendship with honesty, vulnerability, laughter, and prayer. When I'm on struggle street, she's often the first woman I call. When I fail to silence the haters and let their screams in, she reminds me to cry out to the King. When I'm nervous or scared, I usually send her a text explaining the situation and asking for prayer. She has encouraged me to pursue counseling when I couldn't move past a hard situation. After my husband, she has been the greatest supporter of my dreams. She's not only part of my tribe; she plays a key role at the table of my heart. She speaks encouragement when I'm cloaked in fear, cries with me over sorrow, celebrates my victories, and, most notably, uses her skills, abilities, and passions to partner with me as I reach my dreams.

After nearly a year of teaching a Bible study that she drove over an hour to attend each week, I asked her if she could tote along her keyboard to sing sweet melodies over women as they wrote their prayers in journals and shared in Holy Communion. She obliged. I taught and she sang. She did what I could not (and probably should not), making the experience for the precious women in the study that much sweeter. After that first night of schlepping her keyboard to Bible study, I asked her to come again, and for the past two years she has played nearly every time I have taught. My dream of serving women in this capacity has been possible because of her gifts and time. I could not imagine my life or dreams without her. She is woven into the fabric of my dreams, and I couldn't be happier. I can say with certainty that without her indispensable support and companionship, I would not be the dreamer I am today.

You and I are built for healthy, life-giving friendships. Friendships where two people feel they are seen and heard in a way that feels satisfying and safe for both, with no lick of manipulation, codependency, fear, bullying, shaming, isolating, blaming, jealousy, or lying. I'm talking about consistent, encouraging, and vulnerable friendships that invite each of us to become the best version of ourself—the woman God intended, the woman who pursues her dreams and lives the life God created her for.

Our dear friends play an essential part in the story of our dreams, one so necessary and crucial as we chase the dreams that beat in our hearts. Our friends come to our aid and help us meet felt needs. They lift us up when we feel we can't go on. These dear friends, active in our tribe, are ready to give us a blessing. They don't withhold love and encouragement but boldly offer us a blessing that speaks straight to our heart.

Friends remind us of the truth about who we are and who we are becoming.

Acquaintances or casual friends may cause us to question our next steps or our wild plans with questions such as "Well, why would you want to do *that*?" Or "What if you fail? What will people think? Aren't you afraid?" Seemingly well-meaning questions can feel like condescending comments from those around you. But when a dear friend who knows your heart, personality, strengths, and dreams speaks a blessing over you, it reminds you that you were created to dream, to write, to dance, to lead, to do whatever it is that you were born to do. When we receive blessings from a friend, it's often the bold truth we need to hear that drowns out the haters' words and the lies we believe. Friends remind us of the truth about who we are and who we are becoming.

In the same way that our friends bless us in our journeys, may we never underestimate the power of our words to bless and encourage our dear friends. As our friends play a crucial role in our dreams, we simultaneously play a crucial role in their journey toward the dreams that beat in their hearts. It's a two-way street. We were built for a thriving, vibrant relationship with God *and* one another. No doubt about it.

Not only do dear friends bless one another; they share in one another's joy as if it was their own. This may sound easy to do, but when we're suffering through the most difficult days of our lives, it can feel gut-wrenching to witness our friends experience and embrace victory—something we don't possess yet.

It's hard to celebrate the dream coming true for the friend who's having a baby when we've struggled with infertility for years. It's hard to celebrate the dream coming true for the friend who opened up her business with success when we can't get ours off the ground. It's hard to celebrate the dream coming true for the friend who got a bonus at her dream job when we struggle to pull ourselves out of bed for the job we have. It's hard to celebrate the dream coming true for the friend who got engaged when we are still reeling from our awful divorce and wondering if someone will love us as we are.

A good friend doesn't allow her own sorrow to sabotage the victory of another. We celebrate one another, and our own souls are blessed as we choose to be a conduit of joy to those we cherish. It takes an enormous amount of humility to celebrate the joys of another when we feel like we deserve what she has, but we must remember that our journey is unique, sometimes messy, and directed by the Holy of Holies. We can trust His timing and plan. May we accept the role God has for us to play in the lives of those we cherish, our dear friends. May we love incredibly well, remembering that love is sacrificial in nature and full of generosity, peace, encouragement, and hope. In every season as we receive the kindness, encouragement, blessing, and joy of our dear friends, may we eagerly play the role God has for us in the lives of others. Sometimes that role may be more significant than we realize, as we see in Moses' story.

Don't Go Alone

Our man Moses partnered with the Divine for dreams that would affect not only himself but also an entire nation, and God, in His goodness, gave Moses a companion for the journey: Aaron. Their relationship was honest and vulnerable, and they depended on each other to see the dream of freedom come to pass. We first read of their friendship in Exodus 4:

> *²⁷Now the LORD had said to Aaron, "Go out into the wilderness to meet Moses." So Aaron went and met Moses at the mountain of God, and he embraced him. ²⁸Moses then told Aaron everything the LORD had commanded him to say. And he told him about the miraculous signs the LORD had commanded him to perform.*
>
> *²⁹Then Moses and Aaron returned to Egypt and called all the elders of Israel together. ³⁰Aaron told them everything the LORD had told Moses, and Moses performed the miraculous signs as they watched. ³¹Then the people of Israel were convinced that the LORD had sent Moses and Aaron. When they heard that the LORD was concerned about them and had seen their misery, they bowed down and worshiped.*
>
> *(Exodus 4:27-31)*

The grand destiny God orchestrated for Aaron included journeying alongside Moses to lead the Israelites to freedom. God allowed Moses to have a companion who would serve him unlike any other—a brother and friend he could be honest with and count on, whose own gifts and strengths would accommodate for Moses' weaknesses.

As we read earlier in Exodus 5, Moses and Aaron addressed Pharaoh, which led to the brick-and-straw fiasco that made the lives of the Hebrew slaves even more miserable. The two freedom fighters were discouraged, but God was at work in their hearts as He hardened Pharaoh's heart. Then in Exodus 6 and 7, we see Moses vulnerable about his weakness to speak up:

> ⁶:²⁸*When the* L*ORD* *spoke to Moses in the land of Egypt,* ²⁹*he said to him, "I am the* L*ORD! Tell Pharaoh, the king of Egypt, everything I am telling you."* ³⁰*But Moses argued with the* L*ORD, saying, "I can't do it! I'm such a clumsy speaker! Why should Pharaoh listen to me?"*
>
> ⁷:¹*Then the* L*ORD* *said to Moses, "Pay close attention to this. I will make you seem like God to Pharaoh, and your brother, Aaron, will be your prophet.* ²*Tell Aaron everything I command you, and Aaron must command Pharaoh to let the people of Israel leave his country.* ³*But I will make Pharaoh's heart stubborn so I can multiply my miraculous signs and wonders in the land of Egypt.* ⁴*Even then Pharaoh will refuse to listen to you. So I will bring down my fist on Egypt. Then I will rescue my forces—my people, the Israelites—from the land of Egypt with great acts of judgment.* ⁵*When I raise my powerful hand and bring out the Israelites, the Egyptians will know that I am the* L*ORD."*
>
> ⁶*So Moses and Aaron did just as the Lord had commanded them.* ⁷*Moses was eighty years old, and Aaron was eighty-three when they made their demands to Pharaoh.*
>
> *(Exodus 6:28-30; 7:1-7)*

While Moses may have appeared like God before Pharaoh, Aaron did all the talking. They were a team, in it together for the freedom of Israel. I find it so intriguing that God gave in to Moses' implied request for someone else to do the talking when the stakes were astonishingly high. In His kindness, God allowed Aaron, Moses' brother, to stand before Pharaoh and request freedom for the people of God. What a beautiful example of God using two men to see dreams come to pass as they exercised their own strengths and complemented each other's gifts. If you do not have a companion to walk alongside you as you pursue your God-given dreams, then boldly ask God for someone who can bring the gifts and skills where you may be weak or lacking.

Our dreams will nearly always require the encouragement, vulnerability, and companionship of another.

Our dreams will nearly always require the encouragement, vulnerability, and companionship of another. When our dreams become reality it is not because we single-handedly made it happen. It is because we accepted the strengths, gifts, and resources of one or more dear friends to benefit and bless us. It is because we were reminded to silence the haters and share the dream with those we can trust. May those who bless us on the journey of our dreams be immeasurably blessed. And as we bless, encourage, and serve the dear friends in our lives who are pursuing their own dreams, I pray you and I will be refreshed. One thing is sure: as we partner with God and friends we will witness His handiwork displayed through our dreams.

6

Good Ole Days

6

Good Ole Days

While folding clothes or washing dishes I often pop in earbuds and listen to my favorite podcasts. Recently on one of my go-to podcasts the host asked her guest about her rise to fame as a singer and songwriter. The guest, Amanda Sudano-Ramirez, gracefully shared childhood memories in which she sang in front of family members as well as her decision to pursue music after college. She knew she was built to sing and wondered what it would be like to make a career out of it. In her twenties she moved back to Nashville where her parents were living and took any gig she could get. As open door led to open door, she recalled playing in odd towns, sleeping on many buses, and doing whatever she could to keep the dream alive. In that season of small beginnings, her mother reminded her that someday these would be the "good ole days." It was a kind reminder to her daughter that she wouldn't ever have the simple days back. One day she might make it big, and the days of small-time singing would be a gift—sweet days to remember.[1]

Today this woman travels the world and sings in front of sold-out crowds. She cultivated her God-given gift, sacrificed much, and clocked her hours to do what she loves to do. She has seen God's hand in her life, leading and guiding her every step of the way to see her dreams become reality.

For the dreamer who is forward thinking, always striving to build or expand her dreams, it's important to remember that our current days, the ones filled with all kinds of hustling and fueled by passion, are good. They are to be celebrated. Healthy reflection can keep our eyes excited for what is ahead while allowing our hearts to savor our current reality.

I am one to fall prey to discouragement if I don't see things moving along at a peppy pace, but I am missing out in big ways if I don't savor the days I'm living in now. Both the good and bad days have something to teach us, proving that we are alive and trotting along in the destiny God has for us. They may not be what we've hoped and dreamed—yet. But someday they might be; and when those days come, we will most likely look back on the good ole days with fondness. How much sweeter would it be to enjoy those days now, knowing full well everything is going to work out—or even if it doesn't, that the Lord is gracious to lead us on to new ventures? However tedious or frustrating they may be, we can enjoy the good ole days right now in this very season. We won't ever have them back. We can't go backward, only forward. Today will never come again.

I get it, the future looks so delicious; a future of dreams redeemed and made plain in reality sounds so good that you want it all to happen right this minute. But the journey to our dreams is awfully sweet and undeniably difficult. We must keep in mind as we journey toward our dreams that they most likely will require more time, money, responsibility for others, and disappointment. The woman who dreams is no stranger to sacrifice, and the road can be impossibly hard and long. So, why not savor the good ole days now? Remember, our good Father is present in it all—able to teach us, mold us, and make us more like Himself.

In the days when the stakes aren't terribly high, we can bathe in the bathwater of discouragement from the realization that things aren't exactly as we hoped they would be, or we can breathe deep and be reminded that our God is always at work behind the scenes, crafting us and perfecting the time for our God-sized dreams to happen as He plans, which is always far greater than the plans and timeline we have for ourselves. I know this well from personal experience.

Sip and Savor

After ten years of full-time work, I spent most of my days at home nursing a little one, dropping off and picking up my older son from school, and smacking the keys of my keyboard with all the gumption I had to inform women that they are not alone, God is near, and He is for them no matter what failures or defeats they struggle with. On the weekends, I would enjoy the opportunity to share with women face-to-face about the goodness of Jesus to each of us.

On one occasion, I spoke at a women's leadership gathering, and as I was about to leave, a gal caught me and said, "My friends and I are joining your Bible study."

"You must have me mistaken with someone else. I don't teach a Bible study," I replied.

With confidence she fired back, "We are so excited! We'll see you there."

In my heart of hearts, I heard the whisper, "Do it." As I wondered where I would start a Bible study, I felt that it wasn't supposed to be a gathering at my home. I wasn't quite sure where I would have it, but by golly I was going to do it somehow, someway.

A week later I was having dinner at a friend's restaurant where he is both the executive chef and owner. His restaurant, The Table, sports industrial accents, a subway tile backsplash, and two old ladders with Edison bulbs strung between them to make unique lighting fixtures. A twenty-two-seat communal table spanning nearly the entire length of the restaurant anchors the space and hints at its mission: to gather strangers at the table and nourish their bellies as equals. It's hands down the place to be, and the food is the bee's knees.

I utterly adore the chef and his wife, who stepped out in faith to open The Table. After years of working in other people's kitchens, my friend opened a place that reflects his journey, style, and commitment to community. He and his wife are friends who have become like family to me and my husband. They are dreamers, entrepreneurs, and risk takers who live a life of generosity that inspires those around them.

On a busy Friday night, not long after they opened the restaurant, I noshed on medium rare flank steak and ricotta gnocchi with my husband and another couple. The chef popped by our table for a minute to say a quick hello, and the thought popped into my head, "What if I have Bible study here?" The very next second I asked him if I could occupy the restaurant on its only night off, Sunday. As he walked away, he called back, "I'll make you a key."

A couple months later, I invited women to Sip and Savor, a Bible study held at The Table. The chef prepared beet and chevre salad, delicata squash bruschetta, and a goat's milk and Gouda cheese platter. I arrived, alone, to set out glasses, water jugs, plates, and silverware, praying over every seat as I eagerly waited for a handful of gals to join me.

In the early days, about twenty women met me on Sunday nights at The Table. As the weather warmed up, it dwindled down to about twelve. In the first half hour, we ate and simply enjoyed one another's company. I shared for forty minutes on everything from relationships to shame to forgiveness. We ended with discussion and prayer. It wasn't rocket science. It was basic, simple, delicious, and honest. I had no idea that I was living in my own little good ole days.

After a year of Sip, I posted on social media an invitation for those who had never entertained the idea of Bible study. I asked them to give it a try, and you know what? The women who saw my post took me up on it. What started with 20 women jumped to 70 women, and within a month it jumped again to 140 women. Last year, Sip served over 350 women with the invitation to gather, care for one another, and walk in the fullness of God. The increase in attendance brought an increased need to serve the souls of our precious women. With a growing leadership team and expanded responsibilities, it was no longer a small operation but a hold-on-tight, here-we-go, let's-do-this kind of situation. What started out as a simple Bible study turned into a full-fledged women's ministry over time, and I wouldn't trade it for anything. Not a thing.

Simple days may be full of big dreams, but the magic is in the plans and pace. One step in front of the other makes for real progress. We can't outsource, pass on, or deny the progress required to make a dream come true. The steps may be small, but sister, take 'em. That doggone progress is worth celebrating.

Praise the Progress

Recently, I plopped myself on the couch bright and early to watch the Wimbledon ladies final match. Serena Williams, the twenty-three-time Grand Slam champion tennis star was up against German standout Angelique Kerber. I held my breath nearly the entire time as

I rooted on my girl Serena! This woman, the greatest athlete of all time (in my humble opinion), had a baby ten months ago and was back on the court looking fly. This is the same woman who won her last Grand Slam title while three months pregnant. She took nearly a year off during her pregnancy and postpartum months. The woman needed it.

Sadly, after Serena birthed her sweet baby girl via C-section, she had a pulmonary embolism. Small blood clots had formed in her lungs. After that, her cesarean section stitches came apart due to heavy coughing from the blood clots. Days after, the medications she was using caused a hematoma to flood her abdomen. She was confined to her bed for six weeks. Not exactly the picture-perfect start to life as a new mama![2]

I can't imagine the sheer physical pain Serena endured to bring her daughter into this world. The greatest of all time, as she's often referred to, was confined to her bed; but once she healed, she practiced. With her coach's help, she returned to the game when she was ready, not a day earlier. She left the game on top and returned at the bottom. Since becoming a mom, she had only played in three tournaments before Wimbledon, and the world watched Serena once again make it to the finals.

It was a dream to watch Serena whip through the matches at Wimbledon and land a spot in the finals, but she endured a crushing defeat by Angelique Kerber. What would have been her twenty-fourth Grand Slam title in the open era was instead a disappointment on the world's stage, but Serena held her head high and praised the progress in her post-match interview. She shared, "It was such an amazing tournament for me. I was really happy to get this far. It's obviously disappointing but I can't be disappointed, you know. I have so much to look forward to. You know, I'm literally just getting started. So, I look forward to it." After the interviewer called her superhuman-supermum, she responded, "No, I'm just me and that's all I can be. To all the moms out there, I was playing for you today."[3]

In a moment where victory was so close, even the great Serena admitted that greatness takes time. She celebrated she had made it as far as she had; and although she didn't win this time, she said that she wouldn't quit. She'll keep going. Because she knows that in tennis and in life, victory is a process that takes time.

We can't get to where we want to be
without pushing through the middle.

It Doesn't Happen Overnight

We can't get to where we want to be without pushing through the middle. We don't jump to the top of the ladder, do we? Nope. (Unless you are some kind of trapeze artist, but even then you don't reach for the top rung at first.) When it comes to our dreams, we have to work for it. We labor, not in vain, for something greater. We climb step-by-step. Without elbow grease, commitment, and baby steps, we won't move toward the dream. Yet with each gain, we can and should celebrate the little moments. It's in those moments that our faith is stretched and we grow, becoming equipped for all God has for us. It's the small wins, the moments of progress that are strung together, that make up the highlight reel of our journey.

James Clear wrote in the *Huffington Post*:

> Rome wasn't built in a day, but they were laying bricks every hour.

The problem is that it can be really easy to overestimate the importance of building your Roman empire and underestimate the importance of laying another brick.

It's just another brick. Why worry about it? Much better to think about the dream of Rome. Right?

Actually Rome is just the result; the bricks are the system. The system is greater than the goal. Focusing on your habits is more important than worrying about your outcomes.

Of course, there's nothing necessarily impressive about laying a brick. It's not a fantastic amount of work. It's not a grand feat of strength or stamina or intelligence. Nobody is going to applaud you for it.

But laying a brick every day, year after year? That's how you build an empire.

You can start small. You can focus on improving 1 percent each day. You can simply put in another rep.

You don't have to build everything you want today, but you do have to find a way to lay another brick.[4]

If we are focused only on the gigantic leaps and bounds in our journey toward our dreams, we might just miss the little moments, the silent ones, where things are coming together brick by brick. Progress can look like the right person playing a significant role in our dreams, a small step up in our finances, or just that little bit that gets us to the next stage or season. It might not be a tidal wave of favor or cash or opportunity but small, seemingly insignificant acts; yet progress, no matter how small, is still progress. If we were given everything we wanted instantaneously, we wouldn't have the joy of growing through struggle and victory to become that woman who is created only through the journey.

When Moses came onto the scene, the Israelites had been in Egypt for over four hundred years. They had come to Egypt when Joseph, the notorious dreamer, moved his family there during a famine. Now the descendants of Abraham had grown to over two million strong. "To Egypt's new pharaoh, the Israelites were foreigners, and their growing numbers were frightening to him. Pharaoh chose to make them slaves so they wouldn't upset his balance of power. As it turned out, that was his biggest mistake, because God came to the rescue of His people."[5]

Think about it for a minute: generation after generation of Israelites grew up in a land that was not their own. They were so far from where they wanted to be. They groaned for rest, freedom, and justice at the hands of their oppressors. Yet their dream of independence seemed out of reach. Where would they go? Who would lead them? How would they get out of Egypt without facing torture or death? I imagine these were the questions and cries that kept them up at night. Scripture tells us, "The Israelites continued to groan under their burden of slavery. They cried out for help, and their cry rose up to God. God heard their groaning, and he remembered his covenant promise to Abraham, Isaac, and Jacob. He looked down on the people of Israel and knew it was time to act" (Exodus 2:23b-25).

We find God's covenant promise to Abraham in Genesis 22:

> [16]"*This is what the* LORD *says: Because you have obeyed me and have not withheld even your son, your only son, I swear by my own name that* [17]*I will certainly bless you. I will multiply your descendants beyond number, like the stars in the sky and the sand on the seashore. Your descendants will conquer the cities of their enemies.* [18]*And through your*

> *descendants all the nations of the earth will be blessed—all*
> *because you have obeyed me." (vv. 16-18)*

God, in His love and compassion, remembered His promise to Abraham. Abraham was willing to sacrifice his beloved son, Isaac—the one he had dreamed for—in obedience to God. And the Lord provided another way to honor Him, a ram in the thicket, which Abraham sacrificed before the Lord. Abraham's obedience led God to make this solemn vow.

Centuries later, the descendants of Abraham needed the divine hand of God to rescue them from their oppressor, Pharaoh, the king of Egypt. Unbeknownst to them, the Lord was already working to provide them freedom. But the rescue would not happen overnight. It would be a plan that involved the hardening of hearts; miraculous acts; terrible plagues; and growth, trust, and brave actions on the part of Moses.

Exodus 6:1-8 tells of God's specific plans for Moses and the Israelites:

> [1] *Then the* Lord *told Moses, "Now you will see what I will do to Pharaoh. When he feels the force of my strong hand, he will let the people go. In fact, he will force them to leave his land!"*
>
> [2] *And God said to Moses, "I am Yahweh—'the* Lord.' [3] *I appeared to Abraham, to Isaac, and to Jacob as El-Shaddai—'God Almighty'—but I did not reveal my name, Yahweh, to them.* [4] *And I reaffirmed my covenant with them. Under its terms, I promised to give them the land of Canaan, where they were living as foreigners.* [5] *You can be sure that I have heard the groans of the people of Israel,*

> who are now slaves to the Egyptians. And I am well aware
> of my covenant with them.
>
> ⁶"*Therefore, say to the people of Israel: 'I am the* LORD. *I
> will free you from your oppression and will rescue you from
> your slavery in Egypt. I will redeem you with a powerful
> arm and great acts of judgment.* ⁷*I will claim you as my
> own people, and I will be your God. Then you will know
> that I am the* LORD *your God who has freed you from your
> oppression in Egypt.* ⁸*I will bring you into the land I swore
> to give to Abraham, Isaac, and Jacob. I will give it to you as
> your very own possession. I am the* LORD!'"

All that God spoke to Moses would indeed come to pass, but not without baby steps of progress toward the destination of freedom. At times, baby steps looked like God's miraculous power on display through plagues that directly affected the Egyptian people. Pharaoh considered allowing Israel to leave but then changed his mind again and again. The Israelites were promised victory but repeatedly encountered defeat.

Exodus records ten plagues, produced by God, to display the power of God; but Pharaoh did not allow the Israelites to leave until the tragic death of every firstborn in Egypt whose family did not obey God's commands. Some process the details of the plagues and assume they happened exactly as described at the hands of God. Some assume these were naturally occurring events that would have been common in that era; and if this were the case, then God would have allowed these naturally occurring events to prove His power to Pharaoh. Some of the plagues could have been references to assumed power possessed by Egyptian gods and goddesses (the Nile River, frogs, cows). In any case, these plagues spoke volumes to Pharaoh and the people of Egypt.

As you read about each plague, think about how Moses must have felt as the plague took place.

1. Plague of Blood

[19]*Then the* LORD *said to Moses: "Tell Aaron, 'Take your staff and raise your hand over the waters of Egypt— all its rivers, canals, ponds, and all the reservoirs. Turn all the water to blood. Everywhere in Egypt the water will turn to blood, even the water stored in wooden bowls and stone pots.'"*

[20]*So Moses and Aaron did just as the* LORD *commanded them. As Pharaoh and all of his officials watched, Aaron raised his staff and struck the water of the Nile. Suddenly, the whole river turned to blood!* [21]*The fish in the river died, and the water became so foul that the Egyptians couldn't drink it. There was blood everywhere throughout the land of Egypt.*

(Exodus 7:19-21)

2. Plague of Frogs

[5]*Then the* LORD *said to Moses, "Tell Aaron, 'Raise the staff in your hand over all the rivers, canals, and ponds of Egypt, and bring up frogs over all the land.'"* [6]*So Aaron raised his hand over the waters of Egypt, and frogs came up and covered the whole land!* [7]*But the magicians were able to do the same thing with their magic. They, too, caused frogs to come up on the land of Egypt.*

(Exodus 8:5-7)

3. Plague of Gnats

¹⁶*So the* LORD *said to Moses, "Tell Aaron, 'Raise your staff and strike the ground. The dust will turn into swarms of gnats throughout the land of Egypt.'"* ¹⁷*So Moses and Aaron did just as the* LORD *had commanded them. When Aaron raised his hand and struck the ground with his staff, gnats infested the entire land, covering the Egyptians and their animals. All the dust in the land of Egypt turned into gnats.* ¹⁸*Pharaoh's magicians tried to do the same thing with their secret arts, but this time they failed. And the gnats covered everyone, people and animals alike.*

(Exodus 8:16-18)

4. Plague of Flies

²⁰*Then the* LORD *told Moses, "Get up early in the morning and stand in Pharaoh's way as he goes down to the river. Say to him, 'This is what the* LORD *says: Let my people go, so they can worship me.* ²¹*If you refuse, then I will send swarms of flies on you, your officials, your people, and all the houses. The Egyptian homes will be filled with flies, and the ground will be covered with them.* ²²*But this time I will spare the region of Goshen, where my people live. No flies will be found there. Then you will know that I am the* LORD *and that I am present even in the heart of your land.* ²³*I will make a clear distinction between my people and your people. This miraculous sign will happen tomorrow.'"*

²⁴*And the* LORD *did just as he had said. A thick swarm of flies filled Pharaoh's palace and the houses of his officials. The whole land of Egypt was thrown into chaos by the flies.*

(Exodus 8:20-24)

5.   Plague against Livestock

[2]"*If you continue to hold them and refuse to let them go,
[3]the hand of the* LORD *will strike all your livestock—your
horses, donkeys, camels, cattle, sheep, and goats—with a
deadly plague.* [4]*But the* LORD *will again make a distinction
between the livestock of the Israelites and that of the
Egyptians. Not a single one of Israel's animals will die!
[5]The* LORD *has already set the time for the plague to begin.
He has declared that he will strike the land tomorrow.'"*

[6]*And the* LORD *did just as he had said. The next morning
all the livestock of the Egyptians died, but the Israelites
didn't lose a single animal.*

(Exodus 9:2-6)

6.   Plague of Festering Boils

[8]*Then the* LORD *said to Moses and Aaron, "Take handfuls
of soot from a brick kiln, and have Moses toss it into the
air while Pharaoh watches.* [9]*The ashes will spread like fine
dust over the whole land of Egypt, causing festering boils to
break out on people and animals throughout the land."*

[10]*So they took soot from a brick kiln and went and stood
before Pharaoh. As Pharaoh watched, Moses threw the
soot into the air, and boils broke out on people and animals
alike.*

(Exodus 9:8-10)

7.   Plague of Hail

[22]*Then the* LORD *said to Moses, "Lift your hand toward the
sky so hail may fall on the people, the livestock, and all the
plants throughout the land of Egypt."*

^{23}*So Moses lifted his staff toward the sky, and the* LORD *sent thunder and hail, and lightning flashed toward the earth. The* LORD *sent a tremendous hailstorm against all the land of Egypt.* ^{24}*Never in all the history of Egypt had there been a storm like that, with such devastating hail and continuous lightning.* ^{25}*It left all of Egypt in ruins. The hail struck down everything in the open field—people, animals, and plants alike. Even the trees were destroyed.* ^{26}*The only place without hail was the region of Goshen, where the people of Israel lived.*

(Exodus 9:22-26)

8.   Plague of Locusts

^{12}*Then the* LORD *said to Moses, "Raise your hand over the land of Egypt to bring on the locusts. Let them cover the land and devour every plant that survived the hailstorm."*

^{13}*So Moses raised his staff over Egypt, and the* LORD *caused an east wind to blow over the land all that day and through the night. When morning arrived, the east wind had brought the locusts.* ^{14}*And the locusts swarmed over the whole land of Egypt, settling in dense swarms from one end of the country to the other. It was the worst locust plague in Egyptian history, and there has never been another one like it.* ^{15}*For the locusts covered the whole country and darkened the land. They devoured every plant in the fields and all the fruit on the trees that had survived the hailstorm. Not a single leaf was left on the trees and plants throughout the land of Egypt.*

(Exodus 10:12-15)

9.   Plague of Darkness

²¹*Then the LORD said to Moses, "Lift your hand toward heaven, and the land of Egypt will be covered with a darkness so thick you can feel it." ²²So Moses lifted his hand to the sky, and a deep darkness covered the entire land of Egypt for three days. ²³During all that time the people could not see each other, and no one moved. But there was light as usual where the people of Israel lived.*

(Exodus 10:21-23)

10. Death of Firstborn

¹*Then the LORD said to Moses, "I will strike Pharaoh and the land of Egypt with one more blow. After that, Pharaoh will let you leave this country. In fact, he will be so eager to get rid of you that he will force you all to leave. ²Tell all the Israelite men and women to ask their Egyptian neighbors for articles of silver and gold." ³(Now the LORD had caused the Egyptians to look favorably on the people of Israel. And Moses was considered a very great man in the land of Egypt, respected by Pharaoh's officials and the Egyptian people alike.)*

⁴*Moses had announced to Pharaoh, "This is what the LORD says: At midnight tonight I will pass through the heart of Egypt. ⁵All the firstborn sons will die in every family in Egypt, from the oldest son of Pharaoh, who sits on his throne, to the oldest son of his lowliest servant girl who grinds the flour. Even the firstborn of all the livestock will die. ⁶Then a loud wail will rise throughout the land of Egypt, a wail like no one has heard before or will ever hear again. ⁷But among the Israelites it will be so peaceful*

> *that not even a dog will bark. Then you will know that the Lord makes a distinction between the Egyptians and the Israelites.*
>
> *(Exodus 11:1-7)*

After every plague, Pharaoh redacted the promise he had made to Moses. I can't even begin to imagine the deep discouragement Moses felt as Pharaoh messed with his head. Like Moses, you and I can easily feel as though victory is just around the corner yet meet discouragement again and again and again. In the midst of God's activity we are saddened to see that what we want so badly still appears to be out of reach. We've done everything we felt prompted to do, but the victory is out of sight once more. The dream seems too far away to grasp. In those moments it can seem that things will never bend our way. Yet the King is still working. The Lord is orchestrating our growth in ways we never could achieve on our own. Still, you and I both know it can be a painful and heart-wrenching journey even when we trust the Lord for the victory.

Years ago when I dreamed of being a published writer, I applied to have my own column in the local newspaper. I felt confident that I was a worthwhile candidate to hold readers' attention as they read their Sunday paper. As you can imagine, hundreds of submissions hit the desk of the editor. A couple of weeks later I received an e-mail from the editor, and I read it with nervousness and excitement. To my surprise and heartbreak, I was their fourth choice. Three positions were available to writers who dreamed of their own column, and I was fourth in line. I was pleased to be considered among the top writers but discouraged that my words wouldn't be paired with readers' weekend cup of coffee. That effort and understanding of rejection was not a waste. I leaned into the Lord, trusted Him with the dreams of my heart, and carried on. We can do that. We can carry on after discouragement like the best of them. Moses did it, and so can we.

After the final plague, Pharaoh wasted no time and forced the Israelites out of Egypt. It was only after the fatal plague that he caved in to Moses' demands:

> ³¹*Pharaoh sent for Moses and Aaron during the night. "Get out!" he ordered. "Leave my people—and take the rest of the Israelites with you! Go and worship the* Lord *as you have requested.* ³²*Take your flocks and herds, as you said, and be gone. Go, but bless me as you leave."* ³³*All the Egyptians urged the people of Israel to get out of the land as quickly as possible, for they thought, "We will all die!"*
>
> ³⁴*The Israelites took their bread dough before yeast was added. They wrapped their kneading boards in their cloaks and carried them on their shoulders.* ³⁵*And the people of Israel did as Moses had instructed; they asked the Egyptians for clothing and articles of silver and gold.* ³⁶*The* Lord *caused the Egyptians to look favorably on the Israelites, and they gave the Israelites whatever they asked for. So they stripped the Egyptians of their wealth!*
>
> ³⁷*That night the people of Israel left Rameses and started for Succoth. There were about 600,000 men, plus all the women and children.* ³⁸*A rabble of non-Israelites went with them, along with great flocks and herds of livestock.* ³⁹*For bread they baked flat cakes from the dough without yeast they had brought from Egypt. It was made without yeast because the people were driven out of Egypt in such a hurry that they had no time to prepare the bread or other food.*
>
> ⁴⁰*The people of Israel had lived in Egypt for 430 years.* ⁴¹*In fact, it was on the last day of the 430th year that all the*

LORD's forces left the land. ⁴²On this night the LORD kept his promise to bring his people out of the land of Egypt. So this night belongs to him, and it must be commemorated every year by all the Israelites, from generation to generation.

(*Exodus 12:31–42*)

The Israelites in no way had a carefree journey to the Promised Land. Leaving Egypt was only the beginning of their forty-year camping trip in the wilderness. It was a very messy situation, but leaving was still the first step of their progress toward the dream.

As we do our part, the Lord is present, available, and contending for our growth toward the dream He has placed within us.

When we set out to do whatever it is we were created to do, progress will be made when we trust the Lord and move forward step-by-step. As we do our part, the Lord is present, available, and contending for our growth toward the dream He has placed within us. And come what may, just as He showed up for Israel, He will show up for me and you.

7

Dust Yourself Off

7

Dust Yourself Off

Once upon a time I taught preschool hip-hop classes. I'm not even joking with you. Whatever silly image of little ones dancing, I mean hopping, comes to mind, it's probably accurate. I was their Barney, and they were my wobbly baby friends. With a prepaid studio space that I spent all my dollars on, I set out to fill the classes with little ones eager to dance the afternoon away. I did my absolute best to get the word out, and I was sure little ones would come in droves to dance to the latest Kidz Bop hits. That was...until they didn't. I had just three children sign up for my first hip-hop class and three sign up for the second session I taught. I assumed, since I had success teaching hip-hop classes abroad, I would easily have the same success at home. How wrong I was. I lost nearly a thousand dollars that I in no way made up in dance fees. I vowed not to get myself into that kind of situation again.

While there are certainly avoidable mistakes, you and I sometimes find ourselves in a place of defeat and failure when we least expect it. When we think everything is going to be just peachy. When we think the best days, not the pull-your-hair-out frustrating days, are ahead.

Failure and hardship are bound to make their mark on any woman pursuing her dreams. If we have a pulse, then there is a good chance we might fail at something we are learning how to do. We might fall on our face a thousand times, but girl, we have to get back up on our haunches, dust ourselves off, and try again. We can ask ourselves, "Why did this happen the way it did? Was it because I assumed things would be just fine without elbow grease and investment? Why on earth was I gut punched when I least expected it?" Whether we want to or not, failure is an opportune time to reflect—to examine why we did things the way we did—rather than assume we just can't win.

Failure can be a gift, one that is inaccessible through victory.

I have met far too many women who feel as though they are doomed to fail. They are convinced they don't have what it takes after they taste the bitter bite of failure. They are ready to throw in the towel because it's all just too much. How we handle failure is key. Do we allow it to deter us? Minimize our God-sized dream? Do we allow it to define our character or sense of worth? Or do we see it as part of the process, a critical step in our personal development and growth? Failure can be a gift, one that is inaccessible through victory. It can provide intel otherwise not offered. It can keep us honest with ourselves, identify our limitations, and give us a better understanding of what we can do when we feel powerless to see change and growth in the pursuit of our dreams.

Goodness gracious, failure can be so tricky, can't it? It can leave us feeling defeated in ways we never imagined and yet be the very thing that motivates us to get back up, trust the Lord with our situation, and move on to what He has for us. In failure, it is absolutely critical that our ears are attuned to the voice of the Father. He is not absent in our failure but is working every day in our lives for our good.

Failure after failure makes us want to collapse on the floor and wonder if we are capable of any good thing, but within this experience is the power to stretch our understanding and give us wisdom that will keep us focused on the visions that burn in our hearts. Failure provides wisdom not only for our own journey but also for others who dream of greater things. This was true for Moses as well.

Try and Try Again

After several attempts to leave Egypt with the Israelites, Moses finally had his opportunity when, sadly, death fell over each of Egypt's firstborn. After several plagues, Moses was given some sort of promise from Pharaoh that he and the Israelites could leave or worship where they wanted, but each and every time he was double-crossed until death came upon the house of Egypt. During that time, Moses had to deal with the hardened heart of Pharaoh and the growing distrust of the Israelites. I can't imagine the heaviness he felt as he prayed and waited for victory. He tried and tried again to convince Pharaoh of God's power to lead and protect the Israelites, and each time he was met with another false promise from the king of Egypt. I don't know about you, but I would have felt like I couldn't win. Even though I would have known that God was for me, I would have found it hard to believe in the midst of such hardship.

Make no mistake, God was at work. He purposely hardened Pharaoh's heart so all could know He was the Sovereign Leader of His chosen people. At the right time, God made a way for the Israelites to leave the land of their oppressors. The Israelites did not leave because of their own display of strength but because the God of heaven made a way when it felt like all hope was lost.

Exodus 13 tells us:

> *¹⁷When Pharaoh finally let the people go, God did not lead them along the main road that runs through Philistine territory, even though that was the shortest route to the Promised Land. God said, "If the people are faced with a battle, they might change their minds and return to Egypt." ¹⁸So God led them in a roundabout way through the wilderness toward the Red Sea. Thus the Israelites left Egypt like an army ready for battle.*
>
> *¹⁹Moses took the bones of Joseph with him, for Joseph had made the sons of Israel swear to do this. He said, "God will certainly come to help you. When he does, you must take my bones with you from this place."*
>
> *²⁰The Israelites left Succoth and camped at Etham on the edge of the wilderness. ²¹The LORD went ahead of them. He guided them during the day with a pillar of cloud, and he provided light at night with a pillar of fire. This allowed them to travel by day or by night. ²²And the LORD did not remove the pillar of cloud or pillar of fire from its place in front of the people. (vv. 17-22)*

Moses did as the Lord instructed and led the Israelites not along the shortest route but a longer one. Instead of taking the direct route from Egypt to the Promised Land, they took a longer route, which allowed them to avoid fighting with the Philistines. The Israelites were entrusted with the opportunity to believe in the God of Abraham. When faced with hardship, they had the choice to stay faithful to their

Deliverer or blame Moses. I imagine a time of testing and waiting was the last thing they wanted after four hundred years of slavery in Egypt, but God was molding them to be a holy nation that would bless others. He knew what He was doing. Not a day was wasted. Our waiting, even in the midst of hardship, is never wasted either.

God doesn't always work in the way that seems the best to us. If God does not lead you along the shortest path to your goal, don't complain or resist. Follow Him willingly and trust Him to lead you safely around unseen obstacles. He can see the end of your journey from the beginning, and he knows the safest and best route.[1]

God, in His kindness, knew what the Israelites needed at any given time. The same is true for us. Even when we feel like we know what is best, we can trust that the Lord knows what we need even if we don't like it. He knows what's around the corner of our lives before we do.

The Scriptures tell us that hard days were ahead for the Israelites. With Egypt behind them and the desert in front of them, they would have trials just as the rest of us do. At times the Israelites wondered if God brought them to the desert to die. Hardship was unavoidably woven into their story.

In hard moments we are presented over and over again with the opportunity to trust the Lord with our failure, hardship, and loss.

I don't know about you, but in all of my plans and dreams, I don't budget any emotional equity for failure, hardship, or loss. Yet in every season I'm faced with frustration, hardship, and failure in ways that I never would have planned. No sane person signs up for a hard season on the road to her dreams. It simply happens. It seems to be an unavoidable part of the process. In hard moments we are presented over and over again with the opportunity to trust the Lord with our failure, hardship, and loss. We may not see how things will work out, but we can give Him our trust—which is our best gift.

A friend who is a singer and songwriter penned these heartfelt lyrics that I belt out when the going gets tough, when I'm sick and tired of trying, and when it feels like everything is falling apart. It's my distress call:

> *Lord, I trust you, I believe in the words that you say.*
> *Lord, I love you, I believe that you'll do what you say.*[2]

We can trust the Lord when we fail—even when we hit rock bottom again and again. Why? Because the story is never really over when we think it is. The story of the Exodus wasn't over when the Israelites left Egypt. It was only beginning. For you and me, things may be far from over; but the good Lord is attentive and sensitive to the needs of our hearts and always makes Himself available to us. His ways are higher, greater, and more majestic than ours. It is by His good hand alone that we will walk through failure and hardship well and become women of resolve, strength, and deep faith. The question is, are we ready to stop making excuses?

Stop Making Excuses

When I decided to blog with intention, posting more than the occasional inspirational post, I sat in my jammies with a cup of steamy coffee in my hand and my computer on my lap. As I opened the tab to begin a new post, I couldn't shake the feeling that everything I had to say had all been said before. Every good word had been said. There was nothing left to say. Someone else could say it, write it, and do it better than I could—and they already had. I wondered if another voice was needed in the space I felt called to. Would I just be another woman trying to do what had already been done? It sure felt like it. I wondered if pursuing my dream would be a colossal waste of time when gifted women around me could pull it off in ways that I didn't believe I could.

The truth is, women were slaying in their fields with class and grace, but it did not minimize the need for me to join their collective call to redemption and wholeness in Christ. More women, not fewer, must pursue their dreams because if we don't, we'll live in a sliver of what our lives could be. I was silly to think my excuses had any merit. Downright silly. Yet my excuses kept me benched for far too long. Can you relate in some area of your life? Is there something you long to do yet have a list of excuses why you can't or shouldn't?

Many of us can list a million reasons why our dreams won't come to pass. Many of those reasons may pass as solid explanations of why things may never work, but a fair amount of reasons could be chalked up to excuses. Those excuses convince us to walk away from the dreams God has placed within us. And those excuses lead to regrets. A life of no regrets demands we chase the dream. Against the odds. At all costs.

Of all the excuses that we tell ourselves, lack of time seems to top the list. This is probably the most common excuse for why we don't pursue our dreams. I get it; I do. We have commitments that already fill our days such as relationships, jobs, kids, homes to manage, hobbies, and never-ending laundry (the bane of my very existence). With so much already going on, how could we possibly pursue something more or different? For goodness sake, *when* would we? You and I will never have a shortage of things to do—again, like laundry (fix it, Jesus)—but sometimes there just isn't an ideal time to start things and get moving. Regardless of what you have going on, it's a choice to pursue the dream that beats in your heart.

Did you know that all of us have the same amount of hours in the day? Crazy, right? The women who slay have twenty-four hours in a day, seven days in a week, just like you and me. You may be muttering to yourself, "But Tiffany, I've got bills to pay and babies to take care of!" I hear you, sister. I hit the gas to chase my dreams when I had two kids at home full-time, got little sleep, and had bills for days. I woke up early and stayed up late. If I had ten minutes to myself, I did what I could to get farther faster toward my dream.

You and I make time for what we love. Do you love watching Netflix? Going for a run? Perusing your favorite store with no intention to buy a thing? I certainly do. Except the running part. The only time I would run is if I had to run for my life, in which case I probably wouldn't make it. That's okay though. I had a good run. All that to say, we make time for things we love. Our dream, God willing, is something that sparks joy and that we truly love. May we make time for what excites us, for what burns inside of us. Even if it's twenty minutes a day, we can do our part and trust the Lord to lead us every minute, every hour, every day, and every year of our lives.

Another common excuse we throw out for not pursuing our dreams is that we don't have resources. We dream of having or adopting a child. We dream of starting a business. We dream of writing a book. We dream of starting a nonprofit to serve the underserved. We dream of going back to school. We dream of landing the job we desire—or being able to quit our job or work remotely so we can be home with the kids. We dream of traveling the world. We dream of opening a restaurant or events center. We dream of becoming a therapist. Nearly every dream we dream about demands resources. Not just monetary resources but labor, connections, and open doors that we can't swing open on our own. For those reasons we assume our dream will never come to pass, and we don't pursue it. I have come to find that our God provides the vision and the resources. As He leads, He opens doors that would have been impossible to open on our own.

Our God provides the vision and the resources. As He leads, He opens doors that would have been impossible to open on our own.

In my own life, I've witnessed God provide resources for my dreams that have stopped me in my tracks and made me throw up my praise hands because the Lord was all up in my business, working on my behalf. When my husband and I dreamed of adopting a child, we had no idea where we would come up with nearly $50,000 to cover the costs involved with international adoption. At the time, I worked at a church and my husband was a teacher. Though we didn't have duffel bags full of cash stuffed in our closets to cover the gargantuan expenses of adoption, our dream was bigger than our limitations. In His grace, God led folks to straight-up hand us cash, while others designed creative fund-raisers to help us cover the costs. It makes me teary to remember the sacrifice of those near us in that season of waiting for our dream to become reality. The Lord used His people to help make our dreams come true.

Some of us feel we are too young or too old to chase our dreams. We wish we had more life experience, or perhaps we feel we've missed the window of opportunity to pursue our dreams. *Inc.* magazine once featured an article about pursuing dreams that speaks to the excuse of age:

> The irony is that we rarely think our age is appropriate for chasing our dreams. When you're in your twenties or thirties, you may think, "I'm way too young. I need a few more years under my belt." When you're in your forties, fifties, or sixties, you may say, "I'm too old to try something new."
>
> This begs the question, when are you the right age to pursue your goals? The answer is now. Whether you're 21 or 61, you can, and should, chase your dreams. While there are certainly disadvantages to being young or old, there are also a handful of advantages. As a 21-year-old, you have energy and passion that's rarely found later in life. As a 61-year-old, you have wisdom and knowledge that was nonexistent when you were just starting out.[3]

For every excuse you may harbor in your heart, I double-dog dare you to imagine it didn't exist. What if you could not be stopped? What if you could not fail? What would your life look like? What would your day look like? What would your relationships look like? Would you be excited? How would that shape your view of God? How would that sharpen your understanding of your intrinsic worth?

Our excuses are just that, excuses. They are to be combated with grit, grace, and gumption, because the dream is greater and sweeter than the most well-articulated excuse. Don't confuse excuses with legitimate concerns. One causes us to shrink back and the other invites us to use wisdom to determine how best to chase the dreams of our hearts.

Some of us feel we don't know how things will work out; therefore, we shouldn't give it a go. The truth is that no one knows exactly how things will turn out when they first set out to see their dreams become reality. If you feel you don't know enough to get going, think of the women who have gone before you. I doubt Harriet Tubman had every detail worked out, yet she got after it. I doubt Mother Teresa had every detail worked out, yet she got after it. I doubt Susan B. Anthony had every detail worked out, yet she got after it. It's okay not to have everything worked out before we start. Yes, have a plan, but let's not kid ourselves: it's *not* a foolproof plan, but let's get after it nonetheless. Let's stop making excuses and persevere. And that requires being willing to adapt to change.

Change

Are you the kind of person who can easily go with the flow when things change? Or maybe anxiety creeps in when your plans change from no doing of your own. I can be a go-with-the-flow girl, but when big plans change, it can throw me into a tailspin if I think I'm going to lose out on what I thought was intended for me.

Change, whether planned or unforeseen, is part of the life of every dreamer. The vision we had of our dreams in the beginning may very well be different as time goes on. Changes, both good and bad, affect how we pursue our God-sized dreams. In the beginning we may have assumed that if we did X, then God would do Y; but when things change, we may have to act fast, find a new way to get where we are going, and trust that the Lord is *still* at work in the midst of the changes. Because He is.

Our trust in God is tested as changes occur. We may grow in ways we wish we didn't have to in the face of uncertainty or tragedy. As we learn lesson after lesson, it's usually the unforeseen changes in our journey that demand our strength and courage—which we would rather not employ on a daily basis but which molds us into women of valor and faith.

In Exodus 13 we see that Moses and the Israelites packed up their gear and headed out of town after Pharaoh finally gave the green light for them to leave Egypt. I imagine the excitement and feeling of relief was palpable for God's chosen people. Finally they would be free from the oppression and injustice brought upon them by the Egyptians. Finally they would start over and begin a new season. All perfect and cheery—except it was nothing like that at all. Exodus 14 paints the picture for us:

> [15]Then the LORD said to Moses, "Why are you crying out to me? Tell the people to get moving! [16]Pick up your staff and raise your hand over the sea. Divide the water so the Israelites can walk through the middle of the sea on dry ground. [17]And I will harden the hearts of the Egyptians, and they will charge in after the Israelites. My great glory will be displayed through Pharaoh and his troops, his chariots, and his charioteers. [18]When my glory is displayed through them, all Egypt will see my glory and know that I am the LORD!"
>
> [21]. . . Then Moses raised his hand over the sea, and the LORD opened up a path through the water with a strong east wind. The wind blew all that night, turning the seabed into dry land. [22]So the people of Israel walked through the middle of the sea on dry ground, with walls of water on each side!

> ²⁶... *When all the Israelites had reached the other side, the*
> LORD *said to Moses, "Raise your hand over the sea again.*
> *Then the waters will rush back and cover the Egyptians and*
> *their chariots and charioteers."* ²⁷*So as the sun began to rise,*
> *Moses raised his hand over the sea, and the water rushed*
> *back into its usual place. The Egyptians tried to escape, but*
> *the* LORD *swept them into the sea.*
>
> (vv. 15-18, 21-22, 26-27)

If you grew up in church, there is a good chance you remember the retelling of this wild story. Whether with flannel boards, the classic film *The Ten Commandments,* or the animated film *The Prince of Egypt,* you were wowed by the walls of water that made a way for the people of God. The change of Pharaoh's heart that caused the Egyptians to chase after the Israelites caused widespread panic, because there was about to be a slaughter. The Israelites thought their time was up because those Egyptian soldiers in their chariots were chasing their tails! The Israelites' oppressors relentlessly pursued them, and they were desperate for a miracle. Desperate for the God of Abraham, Isaac, and Jacob to protect them, lead them, and give them victory. And you know what? He did! Exodus 14:25 sums it up so perfectly: "'Let's get out of here—away from these Israelites!' the Egyptians shouted. 'The LORD is fighting for them against Egypt!'" That is the God of Israel, and that is the God of you and me!

We spend most of our lives avoiding desperate moments. We don't want for a second to be in a place where we desperately need God to show up, but the truth is He is still the God of miracles. Our God is one who shows up when our life is a mess—when change, however magic or tragic, smacks us upside the head. He is ready to lead us through the unthinkable. To Moses on the edge of the Red Sea, He said, "Why are you crying out to me? Tell the people to get moving!" (Exodus 14:15).

God was not absent when Moses and the Israelite nation needed Him most. He was ready, unshaken by the situation.

Our lives are filled with change. Some changes are a gift, full of wonder and awe that makes us know God is a Giver of favor and blessing. For those changes, throw up your praise hands and worship the Almighty. Of course, some changes make us want to climb into a hole and never come out. Ever. You know the ones, the kind that leave us emotionally, physically, relationally, and financially bankrupt. The kind that make us wonder if God is even paying attention to the dreams that beat in our hearts. It will serve us well to remember that in those times, He will sustain us through the tragic moments. He will give us Himself when all hope feels completely lost. We will discover His mighty hand of comfort and peace when we need it. The One who turned a body of water into walls so that the Israelites could walk on dry ground is fighting for you, anticipating the changes in your life, and He will be with you every step of the way.

8

Get Your Head Out of the Sand

8

Get Your Head Out of the Sand

These days when you apply for a job, it's not uncommon for the employer to issue some sort of personality or skills test. Be it the Myers-Briggs Type Indicator®, LOGB® (lion, otter, golden retriever, beaver) personality test, Clifton StrengthsFinder assessment, DiSC® profile, or the Enneagram, employers want to know what you are good at and how your personality would mesh with other team members. Employers hire for what they need, and they bank on you and me being self-aware enough to take an assessment that accurately reflects our strengths. However, on the other side of our strengths lie our weaknesses that, left unchecked and unaddressed, can cripple us as we pursue our God-sized dreams. As we play to our strengths, we must never ignore our weaknesses and the role they play in our lives.

Like you, I've taken countless personality tests, even the silly clickbait ones where you find out what Disney princess you are. I was Mulan, obviously; that whole "pursue what seems impossible" thing is totally my jam. Anyway, after taking countless tests that all gave me similar feedback—which sounded something like this: "You are a lion. You are a high D (dominance) and high I (influence). You are an achiever, communicator, and learner"—by the end of my self-assessments, I was pretty clear on what I am good at. I didn't, however, have a firm grasp on my weaknesses; and because I wasn't self-aware enough to see where I struggled, I slipped again and again. Until I took time to identify my weaknesses (the Enneagram has been so helpful with this), they got the better of me because I didn't see how they affected my choices.

Weaknesses come in all shapes and sizes. They aren't intended to be marks against an elusive perfect score in life, but they sure do remind us that we are, in fact, human—unable to be awesome at everything. That is, unless you are Wonderwoman, who seems to be awesome at just about everything and somehow very self-aware at the same time. While I know the fictional character has weaknesses just like you and me (her hair is not one of them), it would seem that she is, in fact, aware of them since her weaknesses haven't sunk her proverbial ship.

A common question in a job interview is "What are your strengths?" While some may be shy about sharing their strengths, it can become awkward really quickly if we don't have guts for the follow-up question: "What are your weaknesses?" I can tell you right now, it most likely will not serve you well to answer "I care too much" or "I work too hard." Those, my friend, are strengths masked as weaknesses. Don't get me wrong: an overuse of a strength can develop into a weakness, but trying to think of a weakness for the sake of claiming one without true self-reflection can make us look ridiculous. For example, if you honest-to-goodness did "work too hard" and neglected your family and laundry, then that certainly is a weakness;

but at the same time we celebrate a strong work ethic. A sense of harmony is required to manage our strengths without allowing them to become weaknesses.

Besides ourselves, those around us benefit when we understand our weaknesses, because our weaknesses have the ability to outplay our strengths if we don't address them. You may be thinking *I'm not sure how my weaknesses have the power to sabotage my life* or *My weaknesses are hard to explain, and I can't think of anything major that would keep me from reaching my dreams.* But whether we admit it or not, each and every one of us has weaknesses.

One way to identify a potential weakness (though it's not foolproof) is to look at your to-do list and scan the undone tasks. Which have been on your list for quite some time? Which exhaust you as you read them? Which would you pay someone your left arm to do for you? Right now if you took a quick peek at my task list, you would discover that I have not filled out my son's preschool paperwork and turned it in to the powers that be, although they requested the documents a month ago. While I've waited for a magic fairy to miraculously get this paperwork done, it has remained at the top of my to-do list along with the task "get fitted for a new retainer." (What a glamorous life I live. Don't be jealous of my wonky teeth and undone paperwork.) No one would award me for my outstanding administrative skills. No one. It has been and continues to be a glaring weakness in my life. Help me, Jesus. While both of these tasks are somewhat time sensitive, I fail to get these seemingly mundane tasks done in favor of the tasks that have a "glossy finish." It happens to plenty of us. We pick the fun stuff over the tedious work.

In addition to our task lists, our calendars and pocketbooks are usually a good place to begin our investigation of our weaknesses. Look for clues such as overspending or not allocating proper time to complete a task (I'm forever guilty of this). If I'm in charge of making dinner, go ahead and add an extra twenty-five minutes to whatever time I told you it would be ready. No, make it forty. Some of us wouldn't call these weaknesses but rather character quirks. Yet if they are habitual patterns in our lives that keep us from pursuing our dreams, call it by its real name: weakness.

We all struggle in different ways. Perhaps some of us are strong analytic thinkers, but we exclude feelings from our thought processes. Some of us set impossible standards for ourselves or find we are far too demanding of others. Maybe some of us are the get-it-done type. We thrive on achievement. Yet we struggle to operate with others who see things differently, failing to see their perspectives and how they could genuinely provide a helpful viewpoint. We are so concerned with getting things done our way that we simply ignore them. Some of us possess the strength of getting along with others. (I applaud you. It comes in handy at nearly every moment in life.) While we may be amiable souls, we might conform to the plans and desires of others even when we don't 100 percent believe it is the best idea to do so. Maybe we lack an assertive or bold demeanor when the situation calls for one because we are afraid of not being liked. For every strength, often we can discover a weakness that trips us up if we aren't aware of its effect.

I'm not advocating that you and I spend ample amounts of time and energy improving our weaknesses only to label them as strengths; rather, may we be highly aware of them and notice the pitfalls they lead us to before they get the better of us. Who better to help us recognize those pitfalls than the ones who love us most, because it's not always easy to receive feedback that feels like criticism; yet constructive feedback from our friends, family, mentors, employers, and business partners is beneficial. It is a learning experience (albeit a humble one).

How we receive feedback from those we trust reveals how we handle growth. A willingness to learn from our weaknesses can keep us from messes that we would rather avoid if possible.

If we are are disorganized, frazzled, late, and feeling that we can't get along with others, it is worth it to step back and learn from our rhythms in order to identify where weaknesses overpower strengths. Developing new rhythms will help us stretch and grow in areas that normally leave us feeling defeated. To grow through our weaknesses is wise. To seek feedback, help, and insight from those we trust who are further along in their journey is to grow as a woman of faith.

Proverbs 2:1-11 tells us,

> [1]*My child, listen to what I say,*
> *and treasure my commands.*
> [2]*Tune your ears to wisdom,*
> *and concentrate on understanding.*
> [3]*Cry out for insight,*
> *and ask for understanding.*
> [4]*Search for them as you would for silver;*
> *seek them like hidden treasures.*
> [5]*Then you will understand what it means to fear the* LORD,
> *and you will gain knowledge of God.*
> [6]*For the* LORD *grants wisdom!*
> *From his mouth come knowledge and understanding.*
> [7]*He grants a treasure of common sense to the honest.*
> *He is a shield to those who walk with integrity.*
> [8]*He guards the paths of the just*
> *and protects those who are faithful to him.*
>
> [9]*Then you will understand what is right, just, and fair,*
> *and you will find the right way to go.*
> [10]*For wisdom will enter your heart,*
> *and knowledge will fill you with joy.*

> [11] *Wise choices will watch over you.*
> *Understanding will keep you safe.*

Wisdom that is sought and embraced will prove valuable on our journey of pursuing our God-sized dreams. We won't ever regret seeking wisdom. Without it, we may spend much longer than anticipated and more tears than necessary to be who we want to be and get where we want to go. There is no use trying to be awesome at everything because, dear friend, we weren't built for that. We were built with strengths that can be maximized and a heart that can grow, stretch, and learn. Our weaknesses—and we all have them—are to be known.

As we are aware of our weaknesses, we can celebrate the truth that God is still willing to partner with us no matter how much weight our weaknesses bring.

As we are aware of our weaknesses, we can celebrate the truth that God is still willing to partner with us no matter how much weight our weaknesses bring. When our weaknesses get the better of us and set us back, God draws near; and we are able to move forward with confidence that the Dream Giver won't forsake us simply because we are weak.

The Apostle Paul attested to this in 2 Corinthians 12:

> [1] *This boasting will do no good, but I must go on. I will reluctantly tell about visions and revelations from the*

Lord. ²*I was caught up to the third heaven fourteen years ago. Whether I was in my body or out of my body, I don't know—only God knows. ³Yes, only God knows whether I was in my body or outside my body. But I do know ⁴that I was caught up to paradise and heard things so astounding that they cannot be expressed in words, things no human is allowed to tell.*

⁵*That experience is worth boasting about, but I'm not going to do it. I will boast only about my weaknesses. ⁶If I wanted to boast, I would be no fool in doing so, because I would be telling the truth. But I won't do it, because I don't want anyone to give me credit beyond what they can see in my life or hear in my message, ⁷even though I have received such wonderful revelations from God. So to keep me from becoming proud, I was given a thorn in my flesh, a messenger from Satan to torment me and keep me from becoming proud.*

⁸*Three different times I begged the Lord to take it away. ⁹Each time he said, "My grace is all you need. My power works best in weakness." So now I am glad to boast about my weaknesses, so that the power of Christ can work through me. ¹⁰That's why I take pleasure in my weaknesses, and in the insults, hardships, persecutions, and troubles that I suffer for Christ. For when I am weak, then I am strong.*

(vv. 1-10)

Isn't it reassuring to know we serve a God who gives grace when we fall short? We many not get it right every time, but He doesn't pound us over the head because of our weaknesses; instead, we can witness the power of God in our lives to heal, change, and restore us. We aren't a lost cause because we can't get it together. When we are weak, then we are strong. May we never believe that our weaknesses in one area disqualify us from experiencing the love of God or chasing our impossible dreams. We were built to partner with God for His goodness and our joy.

We were built to partner with God for His goodness and our joy.

There are two related habits we can cultivate in order to compensate for our weaknesses as we partner with God to see our dreams come to pass. Let's consider each one.

Be a Lifelong Learner

Lifelong learning is a choice—a commitment to an enduring hustle in the same direction. One woman who committed herself to lifelong learning was Julia McWilliams.[1] Born in 1912, she was a California girl who excelled at sports and was known to be a prankster. She attended an all-girls school in San Francisco and later made her way to Northampton, Massachusetts, to attend Smith College in 1930. She had big dreams of being a writer and pitched manuscripts to *The New Yorker*, but never once was published by them. In her diary she once wrote, "I am sadly an ordinary person ... with talents I do not use."[2]

After college, Julia had a job in a swanky home furnishings store in New York and was later transferred to a sister store in California until she was fired. With America neck deep in World War II, Julia joined the Office of Strategic Services, a government intelligence agency in Washington, DC. From there she was stationed all over the world. While in Sri Lanka, she met the love of her life, Paul Child. They returned to the United States to marry, and Paul was later assigned to Paris for a job at the American Embassy. Paul and Julia Child packed up for Paris in 1948.

On the way to Paris, Paul took Julia to eat at La Couronne, which is the oldest inn in France. This was the first time she had eaten classical French cuisine, and she commented later, "The whole experience was an opening up of the soul and spirit for me...I was hooked, and for life, as it turned out."[3] While in Paris, Julia found herself drawn to French cooking and enrolled in the world-famous cooking school Le Cordon Bleu. In her six months of cooking school, complete with private lessons from legendary chef Max Bugnard, she met friends with the same passion for food that she had. Not long after finishing cooking school, Julia and her friends Simone Beck and Louisette Bertholle created L'Ecole de Trois Gourmandes (The School of the Three Gourmands). Julia, along with her friends, was full of passion and practiced to be the best chef she dreamed she could be.

In Paris, Julia spent her days exploring open-air markets and fish stalls, and she learned from bakers and fine food makers. She was a student, always learning new techniques and how to make the most of seasonal ingredients. She was a learner, and she could not and would not be stopped.

Tamar Adler, author and chef, said this of Julia, "Julia *learned how to eat.* She did not preserve and shelter her plain, perfectly good Pasadena palate by moving to France and then cooking there, then writing books. She let herself taste and smell differently. She took seriously the smells and rhythms around her, and noticed how they changed her perception—and she came to like them."[4]

As her talents grew, Julia was invited to partner with close friends to develop a French cookbook that targeted American home cooks. She was, dare I say, the missing piece of the pie, and she spent the next ten years developing and perfecting recipes. Unfortunately, the publisher with whom she and her friends hoped to publish turned down their cookbook. But Julia and her friends wouldn't be stopped. By this point, Julia had moved on from Paris but remained in connection with her friends as they revised the cookbook in hopes of a chance to publish it. For a second time, the publisher turned down their French cookbook. Eventually, a different publisher took interest, and in 1961 *Mastering the Art of French Cooking* was released.

Julia never gave up. She kept learning and improving, and she saw her dream become a reality. The best part is, she was only getting started. After a short feature on a local television show, in which dear Julia made an omelette, viewers requested more demonstrations by the quirky chef. She was invited back to host what was eventually known as *The French Chef*. The show was met with wild success, landed her a second cookbook deal, and was the first in a string of shows she hosted. By the end of 1965, over two hundred thousand copies of *Mastering the Art of French Cooking* were sold. In 1966, she won an Emmy and landed a spot on the cover of *Time* magazine. She spent the next thirty years doing what she loved to do and learning along the way. It's said that "Julia spent as many as 19 hours preparing for each half-hour segment."[5] She was dedicated to being the very best chef she could be, and she never stopped loving and learning her craft.

Julia Child had a string of jobs and interests before she committed herself to the magic of cooking. Of all her accomplishments, whether it be cookbook publishing deals, award-winning television shows, or even an honorary doctorate from Harvard, she is known for living with a tenacity to learn, to grow, and to love well the people closest to her. What a beautiful life well lived! Julia was undoubtedly a lifelong learner.

Like Julia, we can learn and master our craft, becoming students of what matters to us. It may not be glamorous, but neither is deboning a chicken. Our choice to spend our lives learning leaves us stronger, smarter, and committed to searching for ways to grow.

Expose Yourself to New Ideas

Like Julia, you and I can become lifelong learners by being open to new ways of thinking and doing things, by exposing ourselves to ideas we might not have considered before. I absolutely love learning. I always have. In fact, according to the StrengthsFinder assessment, it is one of my top strengths. I had no idea my love for learning could qualify as a strength, but I'll take it! Actually, let me qualify that: I love learning as long as math is not involved. I mean it. Math is off the table. Give me a BBC special on tree frogs or a PBS miniseries on the history of British royals. Whether it be *Architectural Digest*, a documentary on processed food, a book on the history of American presidents, the art of French cooking, the breakdown of the justice system, or human brain functions, I'm game to learn something I didn't know before. As I learn, I find inspiration, develop conviction, and grow in knowledge that gives me a greater understanding of others and our world.

Years ago before I posted my first blog, I sat down with a friend who was a seasoned blogger and asked her to share everything she wished she had known when she started blogging. She outlined practical steps to help me get where I wanted to be and threw in a dose of inspiration that I honestly would not have discovered on my own in those early days. Her insight was extremely useful. After our initial meeting, we met periodically over the next few years to touch base about best practices, and she always blew my mind as she shared how I could do things differently and more effectively to serve my beloved readers. Before I ever had a book published, I spent at least one hundred hours listening to podcasts and seminars by writing and publishing experts, those who helped writers craft a clear voice to meet the felt needs of their readers. I learned so much by sitting at the feet of authorities in their respective fields.

As we pursue our God-size dreams, it is a humbling act to sit at the feet of others and learn with a teachable spirit. To find inspiration we can expose ourselves to experts in the field and feed our souls with knowledge and creativity; this will never be a waste of our time. We are growing, maturing women, and new insight is a gift. As the saying goes, "Knowledge is power." This was certainly true in Moses' life.

Think about it, as a child brought up in the house of Pharaoh, Moses was a student of Egyptian culture, beliefs, and norms. Then as a grown man, he denounced his position and fortune to identify with the Hebrews. He learned of their strife and struggle and was heartbroken over their oppression. Once he fled to Midian, we can assume he learned the art of shepherding from his father-in-law, Jethro. Even when he returned to Egypt to address Pharaoh (and his learning curve was rather steep given that other people's lives were on the line) he didn't have the military background one might assume would be necessary for a plan like his, but he was faithful not to give up; he kept moving forward with the plans of God. Despite Moses' weaknesses, God saw him fit to carry out the dream of freedom. In every season, Moses was willing—although sometimes reluctantly—to step out and learn as he pursued the God-given dream that beat in his heart.

Exposing ourselves to knowledge and wisdom is a choice, but we can't afford to ignore the opportunity to grow. You and I do not know what we do not know. As we plant ourselves at the feet of experts, authors, doers, activists, teachers, and thinkers, we glean wisdom that is intended to challenge and sharpen us. At times we may have to suspend our way of thinking and doing things to entertain new perspectives about concepts that we thought we had all figured out. Whenever new information contradicts what we have always believed, it's time to ask *why* we believe what we believe or do what we do. It may feel uncomfortable, but we grow as a follower of Jesus when we learn.

It has never been easier to learn about the things that inspire us. With podcasts, e-books, and online trainings, we have access at our literal fingertips to information—much of it free—that will help us to learn and grow. There are folks out there who are killing it in their respective fields and who have something to add to your understanding of the world and the pursuit of your dreams. Many of us operate on just enough information or just enough skills to do whatever it is we want to do. Yet investing in our dreams will reap rewards that we may not be able to quantify just yet; so if we can do better, let's do better by learning.

Once we commit to learning whatever it is that will aid us in our journey, we can get after it just as we would a to-do list. We might even call it a to-learn list. This is in no way intended to stress you out. The last thing we need is more to do; but since I'm a list lover, I've found it to be advantageous to list what I long to learn.

Reading tops my to-learn list. Reading may not stimulate you, and that is totally fine. Are you an auditory learner? Download some audiobooks. Most libraries have apps that allow folks to download audiobooks for free, or you can download podcasts that add value to your journey. Even major universities post audio clips of their classes that can be accessed for listening. Are you a hands-on learner? Find a local class, conference, or seminar that will allow you to get your hands dirty, enhance your skills, and up your game.

If you and I were to add up the five- to ten-minute breaks in our day when we are waiting in line, stuck at a stand-still in our daily commute, or sitting in waiting rooms, it might add up to more than we think. Add that to the zillion hours we spend on social media, and we have ourselves a fair amount of time in the day that we can allocate to learning.

May we be learners who listen, glean,
challenge our current way of thinking,
and accept new perspectives to grow
into the wise women God intends.

An article on Entrepreneur.com reported this on learning:

> It's estimated that Americans are spending 23 hours every week texting and on social media. Imagine spending that time every week on your craft or your personal enrichment. You could speak five languages and be a walking fountain of knowledge by changing your habits and mindset.
>
> Surround yourself with like-minded individuals and try to always take something valuable away from your daily interactions. Many people are professionals in their field and have valuable information and insight to share. If you have questions, ask them! Never be too prideful, for each question you don't ask is a missed opportunity!
>
> Go ahead and challenge yourself today. Commit to expanding your mind, continuing your education and becoming a

student of life. Utilize the world as your classroom, and no matter how big or small, always come away with a lesson. Remember to cultivate your mind so it is prepared to expand, blossom and grow. And share your fountain of knowledge.[6]

Think about it: If we listed at the end the year not only what we had done but also what we had learned and how that shaped the pursuit of our dreams, we would see just how far we've come. I'll bet it would be astounding to see how knowledge and wisdom have aided our pursuit of the God-sized dreams that beat in our hearts. Then, as we learn and grow, we can, in turn, share our wisdom with one another, helping others chase after their dreams. May we be learners who listen, glean, challenge our current way of thinking, and accept new perspectives to grow into the wise women God intends.

9

Stop Scrolling and Start Rolling

9

Stop Scrolling and Start Rolling

So many of us are guilty of it. Bedtime rolls around and we climb under the sheets in our comfy sweatpants or pajamas—some of us with our hair in a bun—to start the nightly scroll. We scroll 'til we can't scroll anymore! We look at everyone's lives—their sweet (albeit sometimes staged) lives in squares—or we read their status updates until we fall asleep. We gaze at their summer vacations, renovation updates, surprise dates, birthday getaways, and fashion choices. We cannot look away! While I don't find it to be a terrible idea to admire another's life, we lose ourselves when we feel another has it better than us and look at our own lives with horribly misplaced disdain.

We are quick to compare another's best moment—one that they are willing to post on the Internet—to our worst moments, the ones where we suffer under the weight of shame, disappointment, and loss. We feel that the woman on our screen—no matter if she's a friend, acquaintance, stranger, or celebrity—has the life we so desperately want. She appears perfect; and if we are in some sort of mood, we might feel we're a mess that cannot be fixed. No one wins in this scenario. Absolutely no one. The person whose life looks amazing doesn't deserve to be placed on that kind of pedestal. After all, she is only human, just like you and me. She is fighting battles we know nothing about, ones not fit for shiny social media platforms. Posts on social media are not intended to make us feel horrid about our lives— our beautiful, God-is-working-even-when-we-don't-see-it lives. Our lives may be far from perfect, full of moments that we would rather not, and perhaps should not, share with the general population; but they are ours, and God didn't make a mistake when He made you and me.

It's easy for any of us to get overloaded with the fitness photos, globe-trotting posts, or makeup tutorials. I'm all for fitness, and I love cosmetics as much as the next girl. But when those things are in our faces 24/7, that's bound to be what we think about and, dare I say, influence us toward a cycle of body shaming. We might wish we didn't jiggle in all the wrong places or struggle with adult acne although we have a mortgage payment and kids or even grandkids (Why you gotta do us like that, acne?). The truth is, if you and I feed ourselves with the status updates of others more than what will actually bring rest and refreshment to our souls, it is a problem—one that we may never want to admit we are addicted to.

Not long ago, my family and I made our way to London and then to Paris. It was a blissful two weeks of time together complete with making visits to historical sights, devouring more desserts than I care to admit (there is a reason the Brits and the French are known for bakeries), and savoring every second as I caught up with old friends I hadn't seen since I lived abroad in my early twenties. I had zero cell service, checked my e-mail only in the evenings, and didn't catch anyone's social status updates; and you know what? Other people living their best life and posting it on the interwebs didn't consume my thoughts. Not one bit. For nearly two weeks I didn't bombard my brain with others' comings and goings, birthday celebrations, beach vacations, and all that we find on social media. I would have never plopped myself in the "I can't live without social media" category, but I was clearly on it enough to be refreshed when I was off of it. Crazy how that works.

Again, I'm not declaring that social media is bad in and of itself, but when you mix what we deem to be the picture-perfect lives of others with our own baggage—however heavy or messy that might be—we easily spin out of control, comparing ourselves to the people on the screen until we are blue in the face. It's not ideal. At all.

In 2015, *The Atlantic* posted fascinating research on comparison and self-worth:

> In the 1950s, the psychologist Leon Festinger popularized social-comparison theory. He argued that people have innate tendencies to track our progress and assess our self-worth by comparing ourselves to other people. That social comparison leads to feelings of insignificance and insecurity. Research has since found that making social comparisons, especially "upward" comparisons (to people we deem above us, to whom we feel inferior, for whatever reason) are associated with negative health outcomes like depressive symptoms and decreased self-esteem.[1]

As we pursue our God-sized dreams, it is imperative that we fight the urge to compare our beginning or middle with someone else's later chapter in the story. Comparison truly is the thief of joy. We chip away at our identity in Christ when we think she has it better or she has more. The dreams that beat in our hearts are ours. They don't belong to someone else to chase after. You—with your unique gifts, skills, abilities, experiences, and pain—are the right person to chase after them. Yet when you feel defeated, which is never a good time to compare yourself to another person, you may feel like others are smarter, more gifted, and better equipped to pursue *your* dream. Listen, she is not! The dream that God placed within you is for you. Never forget that He took into account your pain, strengths, weaknesses, and heart when He chose to partner with you for His glorious work. Comparison will quickly steal the joy of that partnership if you let it—just as the Israelites discovered in the wilderness.

As we pursue our God-sized dreams, it is imperative that we fight the urge to compare our beginning or middle with someone else's later chapter in the story.

Compared to Egypt

Free from the oppressive Egyptians after they walked on dry ground through the Red Sea, the Israelites quickly found themselves in challenging territory. After witnessing the mighty hand of God, they didn't make their way straight to the Promised Land. Instead, as Scripture indicates, their terrain was the wilderness of Sin, between Elim and Mount Sinai. Perhaps it wasn't quite the dreamy place they had hoped for at this point in the story, yet it was their season to embrace—one full of God's providence and faithfulness; but even though God was near, they compared their experience in the wilderness to the oppression of Egypt:

> [1] *Then the whole community of Israel set out from Elim and journeyed into the wilderness of Sin, between Elim and Mount Sinai. They arrived there on the fifteenth day of the second month, one month after leaving the land of Egypt.* [2] *There, too, the whole community of Israel complained about Moses and Aaron.*
>
> [3] *"If only the LORD had killed us back in Egypt," they moaned. "There we sat around pots filled with meat and ate all the bread we wanted. But now you have brought us into this wilderness to starve us all to death."*
>
> [4] *Then the LORD said to Moses, "Look, I'm going to rain down food from heaven for you. Each day the people can go out and pick up as much food as they need for that day. I will test them in this to see whether or not they will follow my instructions.* [5] *On the sixth day they will gather food, and when they prepare it, there will be twice as much as usual."*
>
> [6] *So Moses and Aaron said to all the people of Israel, "By evening you will realize it was the LORD who brought you out of the land of Egypt.* [7] *In the morning you will see the glory of the LORD, because he has heard your complaints, which are against him, not against us. What have we done that you should complain about us?"* [8] *Then Moses added, "The LORD will give you meat to eat in the evening and bread to satisfy you in the morning, for he has heard all your complaints against him. What have we done? Yes, your complaints are against the LORD, not against us."*

> [9] Then Moses said to Aaron, "Announce this to the entire community of Israel: 'Present yourselves before the LORD, for he has heard your complaining.'" [10] And as Aaron spoke to the whole community of Israel, they looked out toward the wilderness. There they could see the awesome glory of the LORD in the cloud.
>
> [11] Then the LORD said to Moses, [12] "I have heard the Israelites' complaints. Now tell them, 'In the evening you will have meat to eat, and in the morning you will have all the bread you want. Then you will know that I am the LORD your God.'"
>
> [13] That evening vast numbers of quail flew in and covered the camp. And the next morning the area around the camp was wet with dew. [14] When the dew evaporated, a flaky substance as fine as frost blanketed the ground. [15] The Israelites were puzzled when they saw it. "What is it?" they asked each other. They had no idea what it was.
>
> And Moses told them, "It is the food the LORD has given you to eat."
>
> *(Exodus 16:1-15)*

Do you see the connection between comparison and complaining here? The Israelites complained to Moses and Aaron about their situation, comparing their worst moment (to date) in the wilderness to life in Egypt. In their low moment, they failed to acknowledge the providence and faithfulness of God, who was working on their behalf and providing for their needs. Instead, they complained and compared. And at roughly a million people, that was a lot of complaining!

The most majestic moment in this passage, when the Israelites witnessed the awesome glory of the Lord in a cloud (v. 10), reminds us that God is present in our challenging seasons, in the pursuit of our dreams, leading us. When we compare our season of life with another's, we are blind to His faithfulness, sovereignty, and glory. Yet God, in His goodness, reveals His glory to us as living proof of His faithfulness. One source notes that "when God plagued the Egyptians, it was to make them know he was their Lord; when he provided for the Israelites, it was to make them know he was their God."[2]

When we decide to complain and compare, we declare that who we are is not enough, that what we have is not enough, and that even God Himself, at times, is not enough. Our comparison undercuts the glory of His presence and goodness in our lives, which often leads to jealousy and disdain.

Don't Hate, Collaborate

While comparison is the thief of joy, jealousy and disdain are the killers of kindness and respect. There will always be another woman thriving in her dreams; and while it is one thing to refuse to compare yourself to her, it is another thing to respect her and cheer her on in her journey—perhaps even collaborate together, sharing ideas, resources, and intel so that each of you thrives in your own journey.

Never forget, dear friend, you are a beautiful woman. You are handcrafted, gifted, and unique. If you haven't heard that today, I'm happy to drop that bomb in your lap. Unfortunately, as we've already covered, previous experiences and challenges can make you feel less than. Other women and men can make us feel inferior; and before we know it, we react. We compare, compete, and figure out a way to perpetuate these feelings.

It's nothing new. The human spirit has been known to compare, compete, self-promote, and degrade others—all to protect self. It's rubbish. It's detrimental to look at "her," whoever she may be, lining up our accolades, looks, pocketbooks, and whatever else against her. We convince ourselves that we look and act better than she does. We self-promote and put her down when we feel we have the leg up. But we aren't competing for an invisible slice of a pork pie. There is room for all of us at the table. There is room for your gifts, your story, your ideas, and your dreams. There is also room for her gifts, her story, her ideas, and her dreams. Rather than demonize another's past, present, appearance, or track record, we can celebrate one another.

Whether it's play dates, the office, the gym, or whatever situations or circles we find ourselves in, we have many opportunities to position ourselves to be a blessing by elevating one another rather than ourselves—by celebrating one another's differences, accomplishments, complexions, body types, healing experiences, and dreams. When we celebrate one another, we become more like Christ, who celebrates our individuality, our stories, and our lives.

Comparing and competing starts in our thoughts and then moves to our mouths. We have to catch it while it's rolling around in our heads, putting it in its place. Each of us must affirm our value in Jesus as a beloved daughter, recall the value of our perceived "competition" by acknowledging she is a woman created in the image of Jesus, and celebrate what Jesus is doing in her. And we *can* do that. We can hold tight to joy, elevate her, and throw kindness over her like confetti, because she is a dreamer just as we are.

My dear friend Ashley Abercrombie wrote on her blog, *Old-Fashioned Truth Telling,* about the rub that many women find themselves in:

> I've been told you are my competition, that we are contestants
> in the game of life, puppets in the patriarchy, fighting for our

place. I've also been told that I am your keeper. That you are mine. But how can I keep you, if I am always competing with you. How can I hold you close if you are a threat? How can we take our masks off and let our guard down when we have been taught not to trust? Sister, silence has made us vulnerable prey. Our shared suppression has fostered oppression. Our silence is not spiritual. Do you realize our power to conquer fear and battle injustice, when we fight it together?

Our differences have divided us, but they can make us stronger, if we are willing to understand each other. Let's be honest, I may not like your politics, or share your faith, opinions, or convictions, but we have common resistance, shared experiences, and well, we're women aren't we? We have gone through hell, suffered unspeakable sorrow, inexplicable pain, inexcusable abuse, unimaginable loss. We have lived to tell the story....

Wherever we lay our head down—a house with a porch swing, an apartment or high rise, a trailer park or public housing, a refugee camp or foster care, prison cell or train track— when we are at our best, we can find a sense of home in one another. Our pain, sin, and shame matters, and it is affirmed and validated when we are together; is there anything we can't overcome? If we speak truth to power, and live to love our neighbor, is pride or greed, racism or sexism, misogyny or exploitation too great for us? No ma'am, it is not. We are found in God, and we belong to each other.[3]

As much as we struggle with haters, let's check ourselves to ensure we don't become like them. Hating on another doesn't bode well for a dreamer. You may say, "That's not me at all," but you know what? We start competing with each other at such a young age that we may not even realize we are doing it. When we were young, we called it bullying; and it still happens today. In locker rooms, boardrooms, and all the other rooms we find ourselves in, we posture ourselves to dominate one another—and it can be devastating.

Let's stop the nonsense and collaborate with each other to see the dreams—yours and mine—be made plain in our reality. That can happen when we support one another, when we serve one another, when we collaborate with one another. When we do these things, we are a force to be reckoned with. Wielding our collective strengths, gifts, skills, passions, and convictions is what changes the world. It reminds me of what Paul shared with the church in 2 Corinthians 10:

> *7Look at the obvious facts. Those who say they belong to Christ must recognize that we belong to Christ as much as they do. 8I may seem to be boasting too much about the authority given to us by the Lord. But our authority builds you up; it doesn't tear you down. (vv. 7-8)*

Paul made himself crystal clear: Don't one up. Don't boast. Allow your authority to build one another up; never tear each other down. We could all use more of that in this life. Every single one of us. When we choose to love one another, serve one another, and collaborate with one another, impossible dreams become possible. The church grows. Justice becomes reality. Dreams come true. Truth builds. And we see the collective hands, hearts, and efforts that God is working through us together.

Just think of Lucretia Mott, Susan B. Anthony, Elizabeth Cady Stanton, and Sojourner Truth. These women—each with her own story, gift, experience, education, suffering, and faith—collaborated to collectively chase the dream of women in America, whether black or white: having the right to vote. Without question, these women changed a nation. They collectively used their forces, skills, stories, pain, and conviction to pursue their dreams for the advancement of equality, justice, and freedom. None of them witnessed the 19th Amendment to the Constitution that afforded women, black and white, the right to vote in 1920. Yet today we enjoy the right that these women fought for. They chased their dreams, believing that truth and justice would win and that women would take their place as equals in America.

These pioneering women could have given up when the going got tough, when it felt like progress was out of reach, but they didn't. They had one another. They had shared vision. Their support for one another was well known among the reformers of their time. While they may have disagreed about smaller issues, they stood together for a cause greater than each one of them individually; and in the land of the not-exactly-free, they were incredibly brave.

From the past to the present, women are working hand-in-hand to make waves and reach dreams. They are all around us, willing and eager to roll up their sleeves and work alongside other women for dreams bigger than themselves. I can't help thinking of my blue-eyed firecracker friend Lisa. She's a foster mom, photographer, and gatherer of women. Last spring she hosted the first annual Girls Only Prom. Inspired to act by the Me Too Movement, she called on an all-female catering company, booked a female DJ, and invited friends who were party decorating extraordinaires. She even got her own mama involved and invited a couple hundred women to dance the night away for $50. The $50 donation benefited the Sexual Assault Center in our city that prides itself on aiding survivors of sexual violence and assault. Women from all walks of life and ages boogied on the dance floor to the best tunes of the 1970s, 1980s, and 1990s. A simple idea that popped into Lisa's mind blossomed into a dream that took an army of skilled women to pull off. I'll two-step to that! It's amazing what happens when women get in formation and work together to see the dream become reality.

When we support one another, we can make room at the table for one another's ideas, perspectives, pain, and gifts.

When we support one another, we can make room at the table for one another's ideas, perspectives, pain, and gifts. We can move mountains, see laws change, start businesses, dance for a cause, raise the banner for what matters, lift our collective voice, and reach our dreams together. Let's not let jealousy or envy get in the way of creative collaboration. Remember, teamwork makes the dream work, sisters!

10

Voice of Truth

10

Voice of Truth

When I need a firm reminder from someone I trust that God is near, that God is able, that God is in control, I can hear Tyrone's words echo in every corner of my heart: "You are called. You are chosen. You are a gifted. You were born for greatness." His words, spoken more than a decade ago, still ring in my ear, convincing me that God is calling me to serve Him with every ounce of my being, to surrender my life to Someone greater than myself, to live a life I love, to chase after the fullness of God, and to always pursue my dreams with reckless abandon. Tyrone saw in me what I failed to see in myself until years later, the woman I was becoming. He spoke over me a banner of grace, peace, and confidence in the God who redeems. He was my pastor many years ago and is forever my rabbi, my teacher.

Tyrone is the kind of man who invites you to be the very best version of yourself. He is rooting for you to win, no matter what leg of the journey you're on. His wisdom is hard earned. He has faced loss, grief, and pain just like the rest of us, and he has discovered Christ to be the Redeemer, Savior, and Giver of Life through it all. During one of the most difficult seasons of his life—wracked with loss and frustration and struggling to find out how things would work out for him and his family—he said to me with solemn eyes and a heavy heart, "The righteous [are not] forsaken" (Psalm 37:25, paraphrase). I'd heard that Scripture passage countless times before, but in that moment I saw a man believe it when his back was against the wall. He held on to hope.

Tyrone is the first one to admit that he isn't the most charismatic man in the room. He was often overlooked for opportunity and mentorship in his youth and college years. He didn't have a champion who called out the greatness that was tucked deep in his bones. Yet he has spent his life on developing the people around him. It doesn't matter if you are shy, outgoing, an intellectual, rough around the edges, or smart as a whip, he makes it his mission to bring out the gifts and greatness that were placed within you from heaven above. He always says, "No one deserves to fall through the cracks. No one. Everyone deserves someone who will cheer him or her on, show up for the low moments, the best ones, and love on the heart."

When he was my pastor, Tyrone had a sizable ministry for a little country church, and it wasn't because of his polished sermons or snazzy worship sets. It was his heart for the individual, his heart for the broken soul to be made whole in Christ. He was convinced that God wanted to do something in you, to heal and redeem your broken pieces, far more than he was concerned about "using" you. The love of God convinced him he was worthy of goodness and grace—and so was everyone else. Man or woman. Black or white. You were worthy of love.

Tyrone isn't the guy who thinks he's the smartest person in the room and everyone should know it. He's humble, not full of hype. He's a listener and isn't waiting for you to finish talking so he can tell you what to do. His kind eyes and encouraging nods convince you that he's listening because he cares. I can't name a soul who knows him and doesn't feel deeply cared for by this man. He is respectful, kind. His delivery, however joyous or harsh the news may be, is couched in love. Even in his correction he leaves you feeling so incredibly loved, without condition.

Tyrone is a firm believer that men and women are equally gifted and both deserve opportunity, position, and second chances. He reminded me in my youth that women make up half the world and deserve opportunity to step into their gifting. This wasn't lip service. He believed it. He didn't withhold investment and mentorship from women simply because they weren't, well, a man. He was the first person who sensed I had the gift of communication and gave me opportunity to speak to our young leaders cohort and share a platform.

At one point, Tyrone encouraged me to sign up for a Christian arts festival where I would be given five minutes on stage to "teach" to a panel of pastors who could provide feedback. Not long before the arts festival began, he was asked to sit on the very panel that I would present to. As I spoke, giving it my all, he looked as though he was holding his breath with wide eyes and a perma-smile glued to his face. Even in his silence, he did everything possible to cheer me on. He believed in my gifts and skills, and he didn't pass over an opportunity to encourage me—even with a silent perma-smile.

Tyrone was not only a mentor to me but also a promoter of my gifts. During one of the first messages I delivered in front a crowd, he and another pastor tag teamed it with me. It was a message about the gospel as good news for every generation; and rather than choosing a young man to represent the next generation, he chose me to stand by his side—an immigrant Indian woman next to a white man, sharing about the good news of Jesus, the news that would radically transform my peers.

This dear mentor of mine was never once, not for a minute, inappropriate, undermining, or disrespectful. In fact, he gave me such a healthy vision for the pastorate that when I later found myself in a situation where I sensed indiscretion, I knew to listen to the inner voice of warning because he had established such a clear vision of health.

I once heard someone describe healthy mentorship between a man and woman as the relationship between Mordecai and Esther. I smiled at the comparison and recalled a time, before I moved abroad, that Tyrone addressed me for the first time as Hadassah, Esther's Hebrew name. He told me that he knew I was born on purpose, not on accident—which for a girl who was abandoned at birth is a powerful statement. He believed that I was born for a purpose greater than I could possibly understand.

If I was Hadassah, then Tyronne was my Mordecai. A magazine article I read described the relationship this way:

> Esther had a mentor—Mordecai, Esther's uncle, adopted her and trained her for many years in the things of God. It was *his* passion to see truth expressed through her life. In like manner, any person who flows effectively in the power of God normally has a mentor standing somewhere in the shadows. Elisha could point to Elijah. Joshua could point to Moses. Timothy could point to Paul. And so the prophets and prophetesses of this hour can point to the previous generation of men and women of God who held the torch high for us.[1]

Yes, for the last fifteen years of my life, Tyrone has been my Mordecai. I have hardly made a major decision in my adult life without consulting him. His wisdom, peaceable spirit, and respect of the person I'm becoming have been a gift, one I have never taken for granted. Before every major job change, before I married my husband, through the adoption process, and honestly through it all, he has been a voice of truth cheering me on to be a woman who chases God with her whole heart and shares the joy of Christ. I am who I am today in large part because of his investment in the person I was then and the person I was becoming.

His marriage to his powerhouse bride, Amy, has thoroughly convinced me that when a husband and wife commit to playing to their strengths and supporting each other without condition, they offer the world a refreshing picture of respect, grace, and equality. Tyrone often credits his wife for helping him become the man he is today. Her gifts have been one of the greatest blessings in his life—and, honestly, a blessing to anyone she encounters. She's fire. Love and power personified. Their connection and partnership convinced me that one day I too could find a man who would believe in my gifts and dreams and would labor alongside me to see them become reality.

On more than one occasion Tyrone said in so many words, "Don't just vie to be a leader; be a learner. Learn from your circumstance, situation, and season. Learn from those younger and smarter than you and those older and wiser than you; and make every day a classroom to develop your heart and mind. Don't depend on your charisma or connections to open doors for you; become a person of high character who can gracefully seize the opportunities that God brings along in your life."

Tyrone certainly meant what he said. While serving at a large church in Northern California, he was invited to apply and serve at his home church, a country church in the small town where he grew up and where I would later meet him. While on the fence of decision about whether or not to leave his dream job in California, he discovered that the dreams of God don't always look like the forward motion that we planned; but they are forward motion in the Kingdom. He learned that God had no intention of hurting his pride; rather, He wanted to kill it and make Tyrone more like Himself: a servant, a shepherd, a lover of people and not prestige. After prayer and soul searching, he decided he would bring his big time to the small-time town, and He most certainly did. I'm just one of many who have been deeply encouraged by his life and his love of people.

Every woman who dreams of greater things needs a mentor who will speak into her life.

Proverbs 12:15 tells us that the wise listen to advice. Every woman who dreams of greater things needs a mentor who will speak into her life. She needs someone who will remind her of her worth, calling, and gifts. When dreams are kindling deep inside your soul, it is the most beautiful thing for another to come along and fan the flames of purpose and pursuit, sharing wisdom and truth. Each of us longs for someone to bring us along on their journey and share their strength with us, even when we don't see the person we are becoming and the greatness tucked within us. If we find ourselves wishing for a voice of truth, we can look for those already in our lives and invite them closer to our hearts, share our stories with them, and listen to their wisdom.

Perhaps you could invite a pastor, friend, community leader, activist, or Bible study teacher who is in your life to speak into your pursuit of your dreams. When you think about those dreams, think of men and women who have journeyed toward their own dreams and may have something to offer. Approach them, ask for an hour of their time, and ask questions. Share your predicaments, dilemmas, and struggles. Most of us won't have a mentor show up in our world without an introduction. Go for it, girl. Even if someone says no, keep asking. You'll never know unless you ask. As the Lord leads you, may you discover those who could be the voice of truth you need.

Remember that a mentor doesn't necessarily fit the definition of close friend or counselor. An in-the-flesh mentor is one who is willing to invest in you, who values you as a person, and who will cheer you on in the pursuit of your dreams; a mentor isn't looking to manipulate or prey on your weaknesses but to invest in your gifts and personhood. Like you, I'm also mentored from a distance by authors, teachers, pastors, leadership experts, thinkers, activists, and the like. This is just as valuable as having an in-person mentor. To theoretically sit at the feet of someone we've never met and learn from their experience and expertise is a choice (and hopefully a habit) that serves us well as we become the dreamers God intended.

A mentor is someone who will be a voice of truth, consistently encouraging you to address the lies you believe about yourself and the fears you have of your future. He or she is someone who hopes that you will grow to even greater heights than they have because they believe you have what it takes to chase your dreams. His or her insight, perspective, and experience is not merely an opinion about how you should navigate your life but a hard-earned bank of wealth, a vast array of wisdom that can serve you as you navigate your current season.

A mentor is someone who allows you to become you. He or she isn't the puppet master of your life but instead plays the role of encourager and promoter of your gifts, skills, talent, and character as you chase your dreams. This person has developed strengths and gifts that you don't possess and can help you identify blind spots in your life that you may not have spotted otherwise. You don't rise and fall on your mentor's approval, nor do you base your decisions on their opinions. A mentor isn't on the throne of your heart; he or she is simply a wise sage who believes in the person you are becoming and offers wisdom when needed.

A mentor is interested in you not for what they can gain but for your benefit. He or she asks questions, listens more than talks, and hardly ever tells you what to do but simply offers advice, which you can evaluate and then accept or reject. A mentor speaks well of you to others and respects your process and your season, even if they don't always agree with you.

To a large degree, both you and I become what people speak over us. What we believe about ourselves is often formed by the words and actions of those closest to us. All the more reason to seek out a mentor who will cheer us on, invest in us, encourage us, and even use their resources to make a way for us. We stand on their shoulders, heed their wisdom, and chase after our dreams. Even Moses needed a mentor in order to chase after his God-sized dream.

Moses and Jethro

Moses, the man chosen by God to lead the Israelites to freedom, had a friend and mentor in his father-in-law, Jethro. From earlier accounts in Exodus, we gather that Jethro and Moses got along just fine. Jethro allowed Moses to marry his daughter, Zipporah, and accepted him into the family.

After Moses left Egypt with the Israelites, word got back to Jethro about Moses' victory. Awhile later, Jethro paid Moses a visit in the wilderness, and from their conversation we learn that Jethro was a trusted voice of truth in Moses' life and a mentor whose wisdom would prove beneficial to Moses as he led the Israelites day after day. With his father-in-law at the camp, Moses had no choice but to share the day-to-day activities with his trusted family member and friend:

> [13] *The next day, Moses took his seat to hear the people's disputes against each other. They waited before him from morning till evening.*
>
> [14] *When Moses' father-in-law saw all that Moses was doing for the people, he asked, "What are you really accomplishing here? Why are you trying to do all this alone while everyone stands around you from morning till evening?"*
>
> [15] *Moses replied, "Because the people come to me to get a ruling from God.* [16] *When a dispute arises, they come to me, and I am the one who settles the case between the quarreling parties. I inform the people of God's decrees and give them his instructions."*
>
> [17] *"This is not good!" Moses' father-in-law exclaimed.* [18] *"You're going to wear yourself out—and the people, too. This job is too heavy a burden for you to handle all by yourself.* [19] *Now listen to me, and let me give you a word of advice, and may God be with you. You should continue to be the people's representative before God, bringing their disputes to him.* [20] *Teach them God's decrees, and give them his instructions. Show them how to conduct their lives.* [21] *But select from all the people some capable, honest men who fear God and hate bribes. Appoint them as leaders over groups of one thousand, one hundred, fifty, and ten.* [22] *They should always be available to solve the people's common disputes, but have them bring the major cases to you. Let the leaders decide the smaller matters themselves. They will help you carry the load, making the task easier for you.* [23] *If*

> you follow this advice, and if God commands you to do so,
> then you will be able to endure the pressures, and all these
> people will go home in peace."
>
> [24]*Moses listened to his father-in-law's advice and followed
> his suggestions.*
>
> *(Exodus 18:13-24)*

Moses listened to Jethro's helpful advice and appointed leaders to listen to the quarrels and qualms of the Israelites. It doesn't appear that Moses was frustrated with his father-in-law for offering this advice but, rather, contemplated the possibility of change suggested by a man who wanted the best for him and his family.

As Rick Lewis observes in his book *Mentoring Matters*:

> The conversations reported in Exodus 18 reveal a relationship of mutual influence. On the one hand, Jethro expressed delight on hearing that Yahweh had delivered Israel and affirmed, perhaps for the first time, that the God of Moses was supreme over all gods. This confession, and his sacrifice to Yahweh which followed, appears to be due to the strong religious influence from Moses over the forty years of their association. On the other hand, Jethro took the opportunity the following day to give Moses some pertinent advice about wise governance...drawing him into some critical reflection. Moses did not take affront at this, but fielded the questions honestly, if inadequately. In response, Jethro gave his candid assessment of the situation (verse 17), pointing out what Moses had failed to see. Jethro's mild rebuke was confrontational, but Moses took it on the chin, presumably because of the solid relationship they shared. It appears that this was a normal conversation for these two to have.[2]

It will always serve us well to listen to the Jethros in our lives—those who love us, believe in us, and long for us to experience God's best in this life. Those who don't condone or enable foolish behavior but invite us to consider what we haven't before. Those who ask questions and are a guide in the process of our discovery. Those who support and encourage us as we live the life we were created for.

Stand on My Shoulders

Many years ago I met a young woman for coffee. She was smart, asked questions, and spoke with passion. She had just finished a year living abroad and was doing her best to acclimate to life at home. She was always the girl to garner support for a cause bigger than her, spending her spare time serving those around her and dreaming impossible dreams. She had fire in her belly and joy in her heart. After graduating from university two years ahead of schedule, she spent time in refugee camps in Eastern Europe, traveled, and started an outreach with friends in her new hometown of Berlin. I tell you now, she has enough giddyup inside her to run a small country.

For the past five years we've spent countless hours talking about relationships, loss, pain, suffering, justice, and dreams. She has shared her story of pain and rejection, and we've talked about forgiveness, not as a theory but as an action to set the soul free. As she has considered opportunity after opportunity, we've weighed the pros and cons together; and she has made choices she can live with. Her heart is wild for the ways of Jesus, and she is a blessing to those around her. She's one of the most curious, kind, convicted, and adventurous women I've ever met in my life. I love her like she's my own flesh and blood, and it's my joy to cheer her on in this life, sharing any strength or wisdom I have to offer.

As I've been mentored over the years, it has been a priority to take what I've learned and mentor others. When I was barely an adult, Tyrone encouraged me to chase after a few middle school girls, informing me that I had much to offer them and would, in turn, be blessed. He was right. The opportunity to mentor others has been one of the greatest joys of my life. As I chase my dreams, one of those dreams is to spend myself on others. Mentoring makes a way for this to happen.

Too many of us disqualify ourselves from being a mentor, an encourager to those around us. We deem our life too small or simple to offer wisdom to another, but it is the way of God, the Dream Giver, that we would give ourselves away. If we've lived some life, chased our dreams, and seen God move in our season, then there is a chance we have something to offer. You and I don't need to operate a picture-perfect version of our lives to be a good enough mentor. Just about every woman I know wishes she had a mentor. May we be what so many of us desperately want, inviting another to stand on our shoulders.

As we pursue our own dreams,
we'll discover that our cup runneth
over as we pour our love and
wisdom into another.

As much as we crave and need a voice of truth in our own lives, we too can rise to the occasion and give our wisdom away, being a voice of truth in the life of another dreamer. We can lend our strength, encouragement, and grace to the souls around us in healthy relationships. We can cheer on another as she pursues her dreams, and we can rejoice with her when she sees her dreams become reality. We can pray with zeal and passion that God would be glorified in the life of the dreamer we've come to love. We can see the very hand of God in another, witness their ups and downs, and be the voice of truth when they need it most. As we pursue our own dreams, we'll discover that our cup runneth over as we pour our love and wisdom into another.

When I hear the heartbreaking experiences of those I'm investing in, I find it to be extremely helpful to answer any shocking statements with a simple "Tell me more." I attempt to soften my gaze when I hear about something that is heartbreaking, because if this dear woman trusts me enough to share her stuff, then by golly I will listen. I will not shame her. I will pray with her and for her, and I will leave her feeling loved—by me and by a good God. I won't offer my tired leftovers but will intentionally give her the time and attention I would so eagerly desire from a mentor.

If I can, I offer my resources and connections to the soul I am rooting for. I introduce her to people who will take her farther faster. I type letters of recommendation and serve as a reference who will tell the honest truth about my mentee's strengths and gifts. If I can offer this dreamer a platform, I will do so—not just with lip service but with action so that she can spread her wings and do whatever it is she was created to do.

Just as Jethro was a voice of truth to Moses, Moses was a voice of truth to Joshua—the very one who arrived at the Promised Land as the courageous leader of the Israelites. Joshua stood on the shoulders of those who had gone before him. He did not arrive at the Promised Land without the wisdom, grace, and instruction Moses had given along the way.

May we accept the gifts our mentors give us, allow their insight to shape us, and become who God created us to be. And as we mentor others, may we offer our experiences, wisdom, and knowledge for the benefit of their journey, their future, and their hearts. It's an understatement to say that when others win, we win. Whether we are the mentor or mentee, we are able to treasure the life and love of another, celebrate victories together, and feel the satisfaction of knowing we have played an important part in each other's lives as we have shared time, wisdom, and truth. It's a reciprocal relationship that's worth its weight in pure 24 karat gold.

11

Refresh Yourself

11

Refresh Yourself

We've all heard stories of folks passing out from exhaustion or developing an ongoing sickness due to stress. You know the ones, the stories that make you shake your head and wonder how on earth that could happen to some poor soul. But the truth is, it could be any of us who packs on too much in one season and buckles under the weight of it all. I totally get it. When things start to go south for a woman who is already stressed out of her mind, everything feels like a chore. It's all too much. Even worse, we feel weak if we can't keep up.

Rather than assuming we need to listen to our body and heart, we do our best to hide our perceived "weakness" from others who appear to handle their lives better than we do. This needs to stop. No one wins when we are so stressed and overrun that we aren't getting enough sleep, taking care of ourselves, or functioning well enough to be able to process our experiences. It is a red flag when even the good things that normally give us joy now seem like another chore. That's no way of life for a dreamer chasing after what God has for her.

At one point in my life, a loud voice repeated over and over again, "Sleep when you're dead. Don't turn off your phone. If you do, you obviously don't see yourself as a leader." In that season, I felt like I had no choice but to buck up and get on board with the theory that I must work, work, work, work, work in order to be fit for my role. It was an exhausting season that lasted for far too long. I didn't end up physically sick, but my soul was tired. In that season I would not have been able to tell you what filled my tank. I saw everything through the eyes of accomplishment: I must do this in order to do that; I must finish this in order to accomplish that. During that time I dragged my poor husband to countless events and work-related dinners, and I often spent my evenings in meetings of one sort or another. You know the crazy thing about that season: all that go-go-go didn't spark joy. I wasn't dreaming of what could be; I was maintaining what was.

Rest isn't just for the women who have
more on their plate than you do,
or the ones running companies,
or the ones you think deserve it.
Rest is for every dreamer under heaven.

Every dreamer is susceptible to feeling discouraged, spent, and weary in her season, no matter if she is engaged in life-giving action or soul-draining labor. Even the most extroverted, energetic woman with God-sized dreams requires rest. Rest—to let go of the hustle and bustle, to willingly stop whatever it is you are doing, to cease from what is necessary. Rest isn't just for the women who have more on their plate than you do, or the ones running companies, or the ones you think deserve it. Rest is for every dreamer under heaven. We may go far and fast, but eventually we will run out of gas if we don't stop to refresh our souls and minds.

Shauna Niequist wrote in *Present over Perfect*:

> Many of us, myself included, considered our souls necessary collateral damage to get done the things we felt we simply had to get done—because of other people's expectations, because we want to be known as highly capable, because we're trying to outrun an inner emptiness. And for a while we don't even realize the compromise we've made. We're on autopilot, chugging through the day on fear and caffeine, checking things off the list, falling into bed without even a real thought or feeling or connection all day long, just a sense of having made it through.[1]

The weight of others' expectations and the expectations we set for ourselves can sometimes be so out of whack that we always feel we are falling short; and in a twisted way, that fuels us even more to work harder, do more, and take even less time to recharge our own souls. It's a soul-crushing habit that leaves us weary and worn out. Our souls cry out for rest, but we smother the screams in an effort to keep up with what we think our lives should look like.

Rest is both an attitude of the heart and a period of time. It is a choice, a discipline, to unplug from all that consumes us. Only in rest are we reminded that what we do is secondary to who we are. As beloved children of God, we rest to allow our souls, hearts, minds, and bodies to be nourished by the presence of God. Rest is not a time to whip ourselves into submission in order to work for love or money; it is simply a time to be. In physical, spiritual, emotional, and relational rest we unplug and have more than two minutes to ask ourselves how we are actually doing. We are often so busy that we hardly stop to ask ourselves if this life of ours is working, if we even like it, or if we are simply in forward motion due to fear. If we stop, what will happen? Who will we be? What will we be good for? It is in rest that we take stock of our souls. We may not always like what we find, but in those moments we are invited to remake our lives and move forward in the ways we love and desire.

There are times when we are so busy caring for everyone else in our world that we have nothing left to give ourselves. We can't think straight. We are beat. Now, I understand that is part of life, and certain seasons are undoubtedly more demanding than others; but when we find our weary souls in cycles of emotional, relational, spiritual, or work-related exhaustion, we must remember that we were not intended to live under such conditions. Honestly, most of us don't always feel like we have a way out. Yet our souls and bodies long for rest, and they won't stop groaning until we give in. This has been true through the ages.

The Rest God Gives

Throughout the Book of Exodus we see that the Israelites craved rest. They craved rest from their oppressors and their toil. They craved rest for their families. I imagine the thousands upon thousands of families in the Israelite camp looked like a tent city in the desert. Nothing permanent. Never fully at rest in their space or place. The rest they desperately wanted—political, physical, emotional, and spiritual—would take them months, years, and decades to find. Sometimes it takes us that long too. Sometimes we ache and groan for rest but choose to run ourselves ragged, overcome by fear and doubt, while our souls scream for rest.

God called Moses to lead His people to freedom so they could enter into rest. It was part of His restorative plan to His beloved people. In our modern way of doing things, many of us feel the never-ending weight of transition and fear that the Israelites likely felt. We think we must prove ourselves, or we find ourselves in a season where we feel trapped by circumstances we can't control. No matter how the hustle finds us, rest is a holy practice that honors the Lord and makes room for our souls to breathe.

One scholar says of Israel, "The restless heart of Israel... represent[s] with fullest accuracy the dissatisfied, seeking heart of all humanity. In the story of Israel, you and I, by grace, will find ourselves (as we really are, not as we may pretend to be)."[2] To rest is to discover and develop the most honest version of ourselves. Even better, to rest is to admit that we aren't always in control (although heaven knows you and I would sure like to be). For the Israelites, rest was to escape the bondage of the Egyptians and refuse to go back. Rest, as we discover, was a needed gift alongside the very presence of God throughout their journey. It would be no easy task to take the land promised to them, and Moses knew it. That would require battle, patience, and an enormous amount of trust in God.

Trust in God would be the difference maker between a life of oppression and a life of freedom. Trust in God would invite them to rely fully on God's plan and hand rather than their own schemes and attempts at freedom. Trust in God would be the ultimate key to moving forward in the dreams of God. Trust in God would lead them to what they ultimately wanted: rest.

No one has helped to expand my view on the topic of rest and trust more than the late Brennan Manning. In his book *Ruthless Trust*, Manning writes,

The way of trust is a movement into obscurity, into the undefined, into ambiguity, not into some predetermined, clearly delineated plan for the future. The next step discloses itself only out of a discernment of God acting in the desert of the present moment. The reality of naked trust is the life of the pilgrim who leaves what is nailed down, obvious, and secure, and walks into the unknown without any rational explanation to justify the decision or guarantee the future. Why? Because God has signaled the movement and offered it his presence and his promise.[3]

Manning knew what trust in God demanded: full surrender of our perceived control. God has long asked His people to trust in Him for the victory. In Exodus, Moses is invited, again and again, to trust God. From the burning bush to Egypt to the wilderness, he has a choice to trust in the Divine despite what he sees. In nearly every chapter of Exodus, Moses is provided with opportunity after opportunity to trust God for the victory, to leave the familiar for that which is greater, and to chase after all God has for him and the Israelites.

Exodus 33:12-14 tells us,

> [12]*One day Moses said to the LORD, "You have been telling me, 'Take these people up to the Promised Land.' But you haven't told me whom you will send with me. You have told me, 'I know you by name, and I look favorably on you.'* [13]*If it is true that you look favorably on me, let me know your ways so I may understand you more fully and continue to enjoy your favor. And remember that this nation is your very own people."*
>
> [14]*The LORD replied, "I will personally go with you, Moses, and I will give you rest—everything will be fine for you."*

Moses longed for victory, he longed for rest, and most of all he wanted a companion to go with him. I can only imagine just how weary and tired Moses was when he questioned God in Exodus 33. Leading over a million people who had a propensity to blame and complain doesn't exactly sound like a pleasant life. I grow tired with just two children who complain about fruit snacks, so I can hardly imagine an entire nation groaning and complaining for rest when it was the very thing Moses was trying to lead them to. The only way they would get there was by trusting God for their sustenance, protection, worth, and future.

This man who left Egypt in a hurry, made his home in Midian, and married Zipporah only to be called back to the very place of chaos from which he had fled in the first place wanted rest just as much as the next person; but rest didn't come without a cost: he had to convince a million people to trust God. The Israelites would have to sacrifice what they knew—Egyptian gods and self-destruction—for God's plans and dreams of freedom and rest.

Hundreds of years after the Exodus, we read of God's relationship with the Israelites in Hebrews 3. The author of Hebrews explains how the Israelites' trust in God is uniquely tied to rest. We read of a people who forgot the goodness and sovereignty of God and, in turn, groaned for rest. They rebelled and hardened their hearts and missed the very heart of God.

> [7]*That is why the Holy Spirit says,*
>
> *"Today when you hear his voice,*
>   [8]*don't harden your hearts*
> *as Israel did when they rebelled,*
>   *when they tested me in the wilderness.*
> [9]*There your ancestors tested and tried my patience,*

> even though they saw my miracles for forty years.
> ¹⁰So I was angry with them, and I said,
> 'Their hearts always turn away from me.
> They refuse to do what I tell them.'
> ¹¹So in my anger I took an oath:
> 'They will never enter my place of rest.'"
>
> *(Hebrews 3:7-11)*

God's offer of rest was not limited to His chosen people, the Israelites. Rest for the soul is for all of us. Our decision to rest mirrors God's decision to rest on the seventh day (Genesis 2:2). Ceasing from labor and trusting God with every aspect of our lives is a practice, a rhythm, that leaves room for true refreshment.

In rest we connect with the Dream Giver as we trust Him. He is the One who makes us come fully alive to flourish as the people we were created to be. The first generation of the Israelites failed to enter God's rest because they didn't trust Him. They didn't believe He was capable of handling their every need. While we can easily feel the same way as that first generation of Israelites who failed to see all that their hearts and minds longed for, our trust in the divine nature of God allows us to set down our busyness and burdens and refresh ourselves in the Lord.

We All Need It

The irony of writing about our need for rest in the middle of a writing season with hard and fast deadlines is not lost on me. Let's just say that I've come to understand how necessary and meaningful rest is. During this busy writing season I also planned a women's retreat and juggled an online Bible study commitment. Add to that kids who have needs, a house that demands cleaning (or it smells like a teenage boy's armpit), and everything else that cries for my attention. During one particular week, with all these irons in the fire, I laughed and cried while eating cold pizza on my bedroom floor at 10:30 p.m. because I had another couple of hours of work before I could go to bed. I fell prey to the idea that I had to do it all. Again, I understand there are seasons when rest feels impossible; but the goal is to arrive on the doorstep of our dreams not exhausted and weary but full of faith with a rested soul—refreshed in the promises and goodness of God.

In rest we reflect and reorient. We reflect on the choices we've made, our aches and pains, our relationships, and all that has brought us thus far. When we stop and ask Him to reveal Himself to us, we see God's hand in and through our lives. We ask honest questions of ourselves and of the Lord. Without a frantic heart or hurried mind, we can identify changes that need to be made to ensure room for wholeness and health. Rest helps to reorient us in our dreams, defining for us once again the God-sized dream and why we won't stop until we see the dream become our reality.

Refreshing ourselves in the Lord allows us to identify the changes that need to be made so we can chase the dream, not on empty but with a full heart.

As we reorient our lives in a time of rest, we rediscover what self-care looks like. So many tout self-care as bubble baths and long walks, or yoga and charcoal face masks—which can totally be a way that you feel refreshed. But self-care also could look like removing yourself from a toxic relationship or giving a firm *no* after you've taken on too much and realize you can't efficiently manage all that's on your plate. It could be finally sitting across from a counselor and working through pain that has held you back from living the life you were created for. It could be mulling on all that you are grateful for and celebrating what God has done. It could be asking others for help when you so desperately need it. Refreshing ourselves in the Lord allows us to identify the changes that need to be made so we can chase the dream, not on empty but with a full heart.

When we take time to rest, we are able to return to our daily lives with fresh eyes, renewed strength, and often a dose of peace and grace for those around us. I'll tell you now, I'm a much more delightful person when I've had a chance to be alone. It often doesn't matter what I'm doing: reading the Scriptures or shouting my prayers; listening to music or sitting in silence; eating a meal or going on a walk; taking a bath or reading a book—it's the choice to shut off everything else and simply be a daughter of God that refreshes me. Then I can return to my responsibilities and obligations with conviction, hope, courage, and trust in the dreams God has for me.

In rest we remember that we live to please the Father. We do not exist for the purpose of fulfilling the dreams of others. First and foremost, we are simply a child of God, and we exist to enjoy Him fully. First *be*, and then *do*. You and I have dragons to slay, families to raise, people to serve, communities to care for, and dreams to chase; but first let us humble ourselves to a place of rest, cease from work and labor, and simply be. If we don't practice a rhythm of rest, we'll miss out on perhaps the greatest gem of our journey: communion with the Divine—which is essential to becoming who we are meant to be.

Who We Are Becoming

It's devastating to read about a CEO, teacher, world leader, or even minister who bullies and degrades those in their way to get to the top, but it happens. It happens when we fail to value who we are becoming along with the dream that we are chasing. My mentor Tyrone would often say, "Talent will get you in the room, but character will keep you there." How true that is. Character matters. There is no way to outsource the fruit of the Spirit to someone else. The fruit of the Spirit—"love, joy, peace, patience, kindness, goodness, faithfulness, gentleness, and self-control" (Galatians 5:22-23)—is not just a good idea; it's evidence that the love of Christ is active in our lives.

It would be a terrible thing to arrive at the doorstep of our dream by bulldozing everyone in our path, elbowing our way to the front of the line, and hurting others by our words, actions, or inactions—all in the name of dream-chasing. That, my friend, is not the heart of the Father. As God entrusts us with dreams, who we become in the process is as precious as seeing our dreams take shape.

I've heard it said that our posture and facial expression when we first encounter someone determine whether they perceive us as kind and warm. While our outward physical expressions definitely should be taken into consideration, who we are and the way we treat people reflect either the love of God or the wretchedness of our own hearts.

We find evidence of this early in Moses' story when Pharaoh, who wanted to remain in power despite the increasing number of the Israelites, sent out an order to kill all Hebrew baby boys. He held his plan, which was a misuse of power, above the well-being of those he ruled. His narcissistic tendencies came through loud and clear when he ordered midwives to kill baby boys immediately after Hebrew mamas gave birth. When that plan failed due to fibbing midwives, he ordered everyone to throw baby boys in the Nile. Even writing this makes me physically sick, yet many rulers both past and present have stopped at nothing to achieve or maintain power.

Pharaoh had no qualms with ridding himself of the perceived threat to his plans. He stopped at nothing in his pursuit of power, and the Hebrews suffered. His plan to kill and destroy the Hebrew baby boys was foiled, at least for a little while, by brave midwives who claimed those babies came too quickly. These women stood their ground, and God was good to them. What a precious reminder that those with dreams and plans of destruction can be slowed or stopped by people who choose to do the right thing even when it's difficult and they have much to lose.

Pharaoh's heart was cold and hardened to the ways of justice and peace. Moses, on the other hand, was compassionate toward the people of God as he pursued the seemingly impossible dream of freedom for their very lives. Don't get me wrong, Moses was frustrated on more than one occasion; but he deeply loved others, and his love and compassion were evident by his continued pursuit of freedom for his people.

Being kind, patient, and gentle is underrated. It's free, and it exposes the nature of the Father. We take these virtues for granted until dreamers who bulldoze other folks in the name of pursuing their dreams don't operate in kind, patient, or gentle ways. There is a good chance you've been hurt by good people, people who love the Lord yet leave you feeling less than, as if you were a doormat to be stomped on. I have too. Yet no matter how someone's lack of character has hurt us, it does not serve us well—or the folks around us—to treat others like that. Here's my advice: when push comes to shove, just don't do it.

Some of us claim we are tell-it-like-it-is, say-what's-on-my-mind kind of women. We excuse our candor and poor treatment of others because "that's just who we are." While I believe that you don't exist to make other people happy, you do exist to love God and others as you pursue the dreams that beat in your heart. Romans 13:8 reminds us, "Owe nothing to anyone—except for your obligation to love one another. If you love your neighbor, you will fulfill the requirements of God's law."

Though few of us plan to destroy other people as we pursue our dreams, our virtue-less exchanges make an impact on others that we would never want to experience for ourselves. May others find the love, joy, peace, patience, kindness, goodness, faithfulness, gentleness, and self-control of the Father because you and I love and serve well rather than bulldoze them in the name of our dreams.

What we desire most is found not in hustle and bustle but in refreshment— in quiet moments where we connect with the One who loves us for who we are, not only for who we are becoming.

If the tanks of our hearts are on empty—unable to give, receive, or even enjoy the simple pleasures in our lives—let's stop and rework our lives. Let's cry out to the Dream Giver for much-needed rest. We were never intended to live a life of exhaustion, defeat, or destruction. We were built to commune with the Dream Giver, to rest in His presence, and to refresh ourselves in the oasis of His love and peace. What we desire most is found not in hustle and bustle but in refreshment—in quiet moments where we connect with the One who loves us for who we are, not only for who we are becoming. Listen to the Dream Giver; heed His instructions to come away, rest, relax, and refresh your soul. Sister, you were created to dream—but never at the expense of rest. Go on and get yourself some rest. Your soul will thank you.

12

Destiny

12

Destiny

Recently I came upon a news story that left me in a puddle of happy tears—really big ones that dripped off the tip of my chin. The now-viral story was about a woman of color who had graduated from one of the most prestigious law schools in the world: Harvard. While in law school she discovered she was pregnant. Now, I've never been to law school, but I have a good hunch that the amount of studying required is pure madness. There is much to learn, and I could easily imagine a sane person ending up in the fetal position with all that studying. Go ahead and top that off with a newborn baby. That would make for a busy, sleepless season. As the news story goes, the Harvard law student was in labor during exams week and still passed her tests. She even insisted on an epidural so she could finish up her family law exam. In her final year at Harvard, she cared for her newborn baby girl. With the stresses of school and parenting, she wondered if she would make it to graduation, but she persisted.

She posted on social media:

> Today…I accepted my Juris Doctor from Harvard Law School. At first, I was the anomaly of my [marginalized] community. Then, as a single mother, I became a statistic. Next, I pray that- for the sake of my baby, I will be an example.
>
> Evelyn [her daughter]- they said that because of you I wouldn't be able to do this. Just know that I did this BECAUSE OF YOU. Thank you for giving me the strength and courage to be invincible. Let's keep beating all their odds, baby.[1]

Sometimes it seems that for every step we take toward our dreams we take two steps back. We win some and lose more than we've won, yet our lives are precious; and sister, you and I are resilient. We can beat the odds, dismantle the systems and protocols that hold us back, and courageously march forward in our dreams. As I read this news story that left me a blubbering mess, I couldn't help thinking of Ruby Bridges, the first African American child to attend an all-white elementary school in the South in 1960.[2] Before Ruby ever took a step into William Frantz School, it was her mother who convinced Ruby's father that she should take the entrance exam to see if she could qualify. Ruby was the only African American child to be placed in the school.

Flanked by four US Marshals and her mama, Ruby made her way to school amid the screaming, yelling, and violent protesting. She carried on even when some threw objects in an effort to strike her down. She carried on even when someone threatened to poison her. She carried on even when teachers refused to teach her and parents pulled their kids out of school. In the end, only one teacher would instruct Ruby—Mrs. Henry, a new teacher from Boston who welcomed her with open arms. Ruby's days in elementary school weren't easy, but with the help of her mama, Mrs. Henry, others, and her God, she prevailed. She didn't give up. She didn't quit.

Over the past fifty-eight years, children as innocent as Ruby have been able to walk into desegregated schools because Ruby went first. Because of the dreams of Ruby's mama, Mrs. Henry, and Ruby herself, others who would come long after Ruby could walk toward their dreams, including the beautiful and bright Harvard grad I've already mentioned. Their dreams, along with those of civil rights activists who pushed for desegregated schools, were unstoppable. They changed the course of education for all students in America because they dreamed of greater things. It goes to show: you may never know what pursuing your dream will mean for those who come after you. Even more, you may never know the crucial role you may play in the life of another dreamer.

You Can Do This

I have a friend who is equal parts charm and pluck. She has this effortless way about her. With long, wavy red hair, sparkly eyes, and a smile that measures ear-to-ear, she's fiery, spicy, and the kindest of souls. She's six-foot-two-inches tall (true story, I felt like you needed to know). She does no harm, pulls no punches, and is nicer than your grandma, yet she has tenacity like no one I know for the things that matter. She's a southern belle living in New York City by way of Los Angeles. She spends her days caring for two little boys, advocating for restorative justice, and writing. She treats those in her world like they mean the world, even if only to her. If she loves you, you know it. Her love is palpable. Outrageous. Generous. Over the top.

In one hand my friend has a white-knuckle grip on generosity, and in the other she has a death grip on liberty—and she won't let go. As Christ has done a redemptive work in her life, she is spending her life on loving others with such an authentic spirit, waving the flag of mercy and grace over their hearts. She's an old-fashioned truth-teller who will speak life into you and fight for you; and like Aaron in Exodus 17, who held up the arms of Moses to help fight the battle, she'll be there when you fight your battles. Your battles, your plans, your dreams—they matter to her. Your life matters to her. She makes sure you know it.

Years ago when my husband and I were in the adoption process, she gave us a financial gift we weren't expecting to help us bring our sweet boy, Lucius, home. A few months after we lost him in the adoption process, she flew up and wept with me on my birthday, a bittersweet day full of loss and joy. Another time when I found myself at an impasse, faced with a decision that I knew would disrupt the status quo and make waves yet also knew in my heart of hearts was the right thing to do, she said to me emphatically, "You can do this." While that sounds ridiculously simple, I needed a big fat reminder that I could do hard things. When she had an opportunity to write for the biggest online faith-based platform in the world, she insisted the powers that be and I connect. She opened a door for me that I could not have opened myself. She is a blessed woman with dreams and desires beating in her own heart, and with a generous spirit she shares her blessings.

You know for sure by this point that each and every one of us was created with gifts, talents, and abilities. With those unique qualities we can be a blessing when we combine our mad skills with a compassionate heart. It may not change the entire word, but it will change someone's world. I once heard it said, "Do for one what you wish you could do for everyone." It's true. We can't do it all, but what we can do is bless the people around us like crazy. You and I are blessed to be a blessing. What we have is to be shared—never hoarded for our selfish gain but poured out as an offering. What God has given you and me is hardly ever for our own benefit only. As we pursue our dreams, one of the sweetest outcomes is the impact it has on those around us.

As we pursue our dreams,
one of the sweetest outcomes is the
impact it has on those around us.

You may feel like you don't have much to offer in your current season of life, but I dare you to look around and identify the folks in your world whose dreams might come to pass if you were to share your skills, gifts, talents, connections, compassion, wisdom, and resources. Who might they become as they chase the dreams in their hearts because of your investment and generosity? Might it be that you are the voice of truth or the giver of resources that someone else may so desperately need? The most valuable gift you have to offer others is your most authentic self: your mind and soul. Might it be that your dream always involves others reaching their dreams? Might it be that your blessings multiply not for your own gain but so that you can generously give them away?

So many of us feel preoccupied by our life's comings and goings that we can hardly imagine we might play a significant role in the life of another dreamer; but dear friend, as we pursue our wild, audacious, this-must-be-God kind of dreams, those dreams will affect those around us in ways we never imagined—perhaps even change our world in such a fashion that lives will continue to be impacted long after you and I are gone.

Your Dream Will Outshine You

God-sized dreams have the tendency to outshine us. They surpass our time and space, serving people we've never met and affecting people long after we're gone. They take shape in ways that are bigger than our understanding of the initial dream, outliving us just as the dream of Moses outlived him. The dream of freedom that burned in his heart affected millions of people and foreshadowed the coming King who brought freedom to us all.

Like our hero Moses, there have been women throughout history who have chased after impossible dreams despite setbacks, struggles, and fears. Their convictions, passions, resilience, and God-given gifts led them to be extraordinary women who changed the world; and their stories inspire us to chase impossible dreams too. Consider just a few of them with me.

On December 1, 1955, Rosa Parks refused to give up her seat for white passengers on a bus in Montgomery, Alabama, and because of her effort—and the efforts of countless other civil rights activists—our nation experienced much-needed gains toward racial equality.[3] Her story is known around the world because she bravely pursued a dream of freedom and equality—one that affected not only herself but also her brothers and sisters and all those marginalized on account of what they could not change. Her sacrifice, commitment, and determination during the civil rights movement are part of just one of many stories that played a part in bringing equal rights in the United States of America.

As a child, Amy Carmichael witnessed another child begging outside a teashop in her home country of Ireland. That experience marked Amy and shaped her dream to serve the poor. She spent the better part of her life, over fifty years, in India chasing her dreams of loving little ones. She took in hundreds of unwanted children and, by the grace and providence of God, fed and raised them as her own.[4] Even after Amy died, her legacy and heart lived on in the hearts of those she loved.

Anne Frank dreamed of being remembered as a writer, and her words have been read by millions. After her death in a concentration camp at the age of fifteen, the diary she had written as she and her family hid from the Nazis in an Amsterdam attic was later found and published. Anne's diary "reminds us of both the Holocaust's unspeakable inhumanity and the child who somehow managed to say, 'In spite of everything, I still believe that people are really good at heart.'"[5]

In her final year at Princeton, Wendy Kopp dreamed of creating a national program that would change the consciousness of a country and start an educational revolution. For her senior thesis, she developed a plan to match teachers—ones who graduated from the countries' top universities—to disadvantaged school classrooms.[6] Her dream became a reality. Teach For America, started by Kopp, has trained over twenty-four thousand teachers and served three million students.[7]

In 1940, Wangari Muta Maathai was born in Nyeri, Kenya. The first woman in East and Central Africa to earn a doctorate degree,[8] she became a political activist. Wangari founded the Green Belt Movement in 1977 "in an effort to empower rural women who had started reporting their streams were drying up, their food supply was less secure, and they had to walk further than ever before for firewood."[9] Through the Green Belt Movement she has assisted women to plant more than twenty million trees on their farms, school grounds, and church compounds.[10]

Harriet Beecher Stowe was an acclaimed writer and abolitionist of the nineteenth century. Though her publishing credits include many books, essays, and articles, she is best known for her novel *Uncle Tom's Cabin*, which presented a realistic picture of slavery and the suffering of slaves. With strong Christian themes, the book clearly conveys the belief that slavery is a sin. The book sold over one million copies worldwide.[11]

Even though Fanny Crosby was blind from birth, she composed more than eight thousand hymns. Known as the "queen of gospel song writers," her most famous songs include "Blessed Assurance," "Rescue the Perishing," and "Pass Me Not, O Gentle Savior." It is said that Fanny "prayed that her hymns would bring people to Christ, and she believed her songs were divinely inspired."[12]

Mary Slessor, born in 1848 in Scotland, was inspired to devote her life to missions in a day and age when women were not encouraged to be involved in that kind of work. After serving for a while in Calabar, now modern Nigeria, she set up a missions station and ministered to the tribal people there, reaching them by way of canoe. One source notes, "Her work laid the foundations for the widespread growth of Christianity in Nigeria today. With her great conviction, she opposed harmful African traditions such as the ritualistic killing of twins in Calabar."[13]

These bold, courageous, forceful women did not take the easy road. They counted the costs and chased their seemingly impossible God-sized dreams. They left the world better than they found it and lived lives of passion, grace, and grit. If they could chase their dreams—dreams of caring for orphans, freeing slaves, fighting for equality, creating systems to serve the disadvantaged, and writing words that matter and change hearts, then sister, so can you and I! We can paint, dance, lead, advocate, direct, teach, adopt, shepherd, sacrifice, parent, mentor, fight, serve, counsel, march, and do all that we dream to do. No question about it. We aren't here to sit down, shut up, and pass time. We are here to rise, slay, and take our place as dreamers who follow the Dream Giver, who is faithful to His promise.

The Promised Dream

God gave a dream and a promise to Moses, and He was faithful to Moses throughout his lifetime; and in the end, the dream Moses pursued was bigger than he was. It outlived him. Though Moses never entered into the Promised Land, Joshua and thousands upon thousands of Israelites did—people who put their trust in God. Before he died, Moses drank in the view of the Promised Land with his own two eyes; every inch of land God had promised, Moses was able to see the promise not just in his dreams but also in his present reality. After he died, the Israelites mourned his death before they allowed their newly appointed leader, Joshua, to lead them. Then they took the land that was promised to them, land they had only dreamed of to this point.

> [1]*After the death of Moses the* LORD's *servant, the* LORD *spoke to Joshua son of Nun, Moses' assistant. He said,* [2]*"Moses my servant is dead. Therefore, the time has come for you to lead these people, the Israelites, across the Jordan River into the land I am giving them.* [3]*I promise you what I promised Moses: 'Wherever you set foot, you will be on land I have given you—* [4]*from the Negev wilderness in the south to the Lebanon mountains in the north, from the Euphrates River in the east to the Mediterranean Sea in the west, including all the land of the Hittites.'* [5]*No one will be able to stand against you as long as you live. For I*

> *will be with you as I was with Moses. I will not fail you or*
> *abandon you."*
>
> *(Joshua 1:1-5)*

In Moses' absence, Joshua carried on the dream that outlived his mentor and friend. He bravely led the people of God by the power of God, and God was with him every step of the way. Of course, Joshua faced his fair share of battles and endured many struggles, but God was faithful to him all the days of his life just as He had been to Moses. In Joshua 21, we read of God's fulfilling Israel's dreams. Here we see that no promise was left unfulfilled; the dream became reality:

> [43]*So the LORD gave to Israel all the land he had sworn*
> *to give their ancestors, and they took possession of it and*
> *settled there.* [44]*And the LORD gave them rest on every side,*
> *just as he had solemnly promised their ancestors. None*
> *of their enemies could stand against them, for the LORD*
> *helped them conquer all their enemies.* [45]*Not a single one*
> *of all the good promises the LORD had given to the family of*
> *Israel was left unfulfilled; everything he had spoken*
> *came true.*
>
> *(vv. 43-45)*

God's plans for the nation of Israel were good, and His plans for us are good too. The dreams that He places within our hearts are worth the fight and hustle. They are worth sacrificing the good things in life in order to make room for the greater ways of the Father. They invite us to rest, to trust in the heart of God while pursuing the plans of God. They invite us to be the most authentic, honest versions of ourselves we can be, and they test us in ways we might never have expected.

His dreams call out the greatness within us. They inform us that we are a force for good. God's dreams for us and the women who've gone before us tell a story about a Dream Giver who believes in our innate giftings, skills, and abilities. He is one who champions the cause and dreams of women, no matter where we come from and no matter what or who has held us back. Like every woman on the face of the earth, you and I were created to dream!

The Dream Giver

Like any woman with a pulse, I've had times when my back was against the wall, and I've had seasons when I've certainly lost more than I have gained. Dreams of a marriage, a child, or a new venture didn't turn out as I had hoped, but all was not lost. I was left with the Dream Giver, the one who loves me, longs for my good, and will never leave me for dead. He was behind the scenes, working everything for good. He was with me and for me, leading me all the way. There was never a moment when I had to fight for the dream on my own. We were in it together. Partners every step of the way. He was kind to me. He held me. And I found abundant life tucked in His presence. In the end, I wanted Him more than the dream.

In our lives we will experience dreams dying, dreams being resurrected, and dreams becoming reality. Through it all, may the Dream Giver always be the One we long for—more than our dreams, more than our plans; may the Dream Giver be the One we are after. I promise you this: the One who created us will always be enough for us. As we place Him on the throne of our lives, we can run toward our dreams with the Dream Giver, never apart from Him. He is the Giver of the dream, our Partner as we pursue the dream, and the One who gives us the victory.

To dream is to trust God with our destiny and live a life worthy of the calling that has been placed upon us. Each and every one of us was born to dream. You and I were built for a much larger capacity than we imagine; we are stronger than we think we are. And let me assure you of this: you are probably doing a better job than you think you are. The Dream Giver delights in you, loves you, and will never leave or forsake you. You are the dream of His heart. You are what He is after. Your life is so very precious to Him; and He wants more than anything to draw you in, love you, strengthen you, and unleash you to reach the dreams He has placed within you.

> *May we never settle for a counterfeit dream giver but listen and follow the one true Dream Giver, who calls us deeper, leads us, and proves faithful even when our backs are against the wall.*

May we never settle for a counterfeit dream giver but listen and follow the one true Dream Giver, who calls us deeper, leads us, and proves faithful even when our backs are against the wall. Let's chase Him all the way home, where one day we'll meet Him face-to-face. From our first breath to our last, He will be our Companion. He will be there on the road ahead, redeem the path we've traveled, and give us victory when it seems out of reach. You and I won't be left alone, because what we need most is what we already have: the Dream Giver Himself.

Notes

Introduction

1. Mark Anthony, *The Beautiful Truth* (New York: Love Inc., 2015), 40.

Chapter 1

1. Amy Parker and Vanessa Brantley-Newton, *The Plans I Have for You* (Grand Rapids, MI: Zonderkidz, 2016), 5–6.
2. Maria Konnikova, "How People Learn to Become Resilient," *The New Yorker*, February 11, 2016, www.newyorker.com/science/maria -konnikova/the-secret-formula-for-resilience, accessed July 14, 2018.

Chapter 2

1. Harmony Dust, "My Story: The Parts Formerly Untold," *Treasures*, January 3, 2016, www.iamatreasure.com/my-story-the-parts -formerly-untold/, accessed July 14, 2018.
2. Harmony Dust, "Dreams Redeemed Pt 2: Don't Give Up," *Treasures*, October 9, 2012, www.iamatreasure.com/dreams-redeemed-pt-2-dont -give-up/, accessed July 14, 2018.

Chapter 3

1. Betty Friedan, "Women Are People, Too," *Good Housekeeping*, August 9, 2010, www.goodhousekeeping.com/life/career/advice

/a18890/1960-betty-friedan-article/, accessed July 14, 2018.

2. Nancy DeMoss Wolgemuth, *God's True Woman*, e-book edition (Wheaton, IL: Crossway Books, 2008), 68.

3. Facts about Margaret Thatcher are from "Biography," *Margaret Thatcher Foundation*, www.margaretthatcher.org/essential/biography.asp, accessed July 14, 2018.

4. "Collins English Dictionary, s.v. "The Iron Lady," www.collinsdictionary .com/us/dictionary/english/the-iron-lady, accessed July 14, 2008.

Chapter 4

1. Exodus 2:17, *Ellicott's Commentary for English Readers*, n.p., n.d., http://biblehub.com/exodus/2-17.htm, accessed July 10, 2018.

Chapter 5

1. S. D. Barbour, *Diversity's Voice: Now and Then* (Lulu.com, 2012), 82, https://books.google.com/books?id=jQ6BCwAAQBAJ&printsec =frontcover&dq=diversity+voices+maya+angelou+haters&hl =en&sa=X&ved=0ahUKEwi0gNCY66HcAhUjGDQIHXCVCD4Q6A- EIKTAA#v=onepage&q=diversity%20voices%20maya%20angelou %20haters&f=false, accessed July 14, 2018.

Chapter 6

1. The Shauna Niequist Podcast, June 19, 2017, https://www.stitcher .com/podcast/relevant-podcast-network/the-shauna-niequist -podcast/e/50594647.

2. Rob Haskell, "Serena Williams on Motherhood, Marriage, and Making Her Comeback," *Vogue*, January 10, 2018, www.vogue.com/article /serena-williams-vogue-cover-interview-february-2018, accessed July 14, 2018.

3. "Serena Williams—I Was Playing for All the Moms," *YouTube*, July 14, 2018. www.youtube.com/watch?v=afh7CYz5M1M, accessed July 14, 2018.

4. James Clear, "Rome Wasn't Built in a Day, But They Were Laying Bricks Every Hour," *The Huffington Post*, March 12, 2014, www.huffingtonpost .com/james-clear/motivation_b_4935330.html, accessed July 14, 2018.

5. *Life Application Study Bible: New Living Translation Second Edition* (Wheaton, IL: Tyndale House Publishers, 1996, 2004), 94.

Chapter 7

1. *Life Application Study Bible: New Living Translation Second Edition* (Wheaton, IL: Tyndale House Publishers), 116.

2. Miguel Villahermosa, *"Lord, I Trust You,"* 2018. No copyright.

3. Samuel Edwards, "5 Excuses We Make for Not Chasing Our Dreams," *Inc.com*, December 7, 2015, www.inc.com/samuel-edwards/5-excuses -we-make-for-not-chasing-our-dreams.html, accessed July 14, 2018.

Chapter 8

1. Factual information on Julia Child throughout this section is from "Julia Child Biography," *Biography.com*, A&E Networks Television, March 5, 2018, www.biography.com/people/julia-child-9246767; and "Biography of Julia Child," *PBS*, June 15, 2005, www.pbs.org /wnet/americanmasters/julia-child-about-julia-child/555/, accessed July 14, 2018.

2. "Biography of Julia Child."

3. Ibid.

4. Tamar Adler, "Learning How to Eat," *The New Yorker*, August 15, 2012, www.newyorker.com/culture/culture-desk/learning-how-to-eat, accessed July 14, 2018.

5. "Biography of Julia Child."

6. Matt Mayberry, "Why You Should Strive to Be a Lifelong Learner," *Entrepreneur*, May 1, 2015, www.entrepreneur.com/article/245696, accessed July 14, 2018.

Chapter 9

1. James Hamblin, "The Key to Healthy Facebook Use: Don't Compare Yourself to Others," *The Atlantic*, Atlantic Media Company, April 8, 2015, www.theatlantic.com/health/archive/2015/04/ways-to-use -facebook-without-feeling-depressed/389916/, accessed July 14, 2018.
2. Matthew Henry, "Exodus 16, Matthew Henry's Commentary," Bible Hub, n.d., http://biblehub.com/commentaries/mhc/exodus/16.htm, accessed July 10, 2018.
3. Ashley Abercrombie, "A Letter of Love to My Sisters," *Old-Fashioned Truth-Telling*, AshAbercrombie.org, March 8, 2018, www .ashabercrombie.org/2018/03/08/a-letter-of-love-to-my-sisters/, accessed July 14, 2018.

Chapter 10

1. Mike Shreve, "6 Earmarks of a Modern-Day Esther," *Charisma Magazine*, June 29, 2015, www.charismamag.com/spirit/spiritual -growth/23661-6-earmarks-of-a-modern-day-esther, accessed July 14, 2018.
2. Rick Lewis, *Mentoring Matters: Building Strong Christian Leaders, Avoiding Burnout, Reaching the Finishing Line,* e-book edition (Oxford: Monarch Books, 2009), 43.

Chapter 11

1. Shauna Niequist, *Present over Perfect: Leaving Behind Frantic for a Simpler, More Soulful Way of Living* (Grand Rapids, MI: Zondervan, 2016), 223.

2. Douglas Kelly, "God's Rest for God's People," *Ligonier Ministries*, March 1, 2004, www.ligonier.org/learn/articles/gods-rest-gods-people/, accessed July 14, 2018.

3. Brennan Manning, *Ruthless Trust: The Ragamuffin's Path to God*, e-book edition (San Francisco: HarperOne, 2010), 12-13.

Chapter 12

1. N'dea Yancey-Bragg, "Single Mom's Inspiring Post about Graduating from Harvard Law Goes Viral," *USA Today*, May 31, 2018, www .usatoday.com/story/news/nation-now/2018/05/31/single-mom-24 -graduates-harvard-law-school/659481002/, accessed July 14, 2018.

2. Facts about Ruby Bridges are from "Ruby Bridges," *Biography.com*, A&E Networks Television, January 18, 2018, www.biography.com/people /ruby-bridges-475426, accessed July 14, 2018.

3. Facts about Rosa Parks are from "Rosa Parks," *Biography.com*, A&E Networks Television, February 27, 2018, www.biography.com/people /rosa-parks-9433715, accessed July 14, 2018.

4. Facts about Amy Carmichael are from "Amy Carmichael Helped the Helpless," *Christianity.com*, July 16, 2010, www.christianity.com /church/church-history/church-history-for-kids/amy-carmichael -helped-the-helpless-11634859.html, accessed July 14, 2018.

5. "Anne Frank" in "120 Women Who Changed Our World," Kara Ladd, *Good Housekeeping*, March 2, 2018, https://www.goodhousekeeping .com/life/inspirational-stories/g2239/women-who-changed-our -world/?slide=59, accessed July 14, 2018.

6. "Wendy Kopp," Academy of Achievement, November 10, 2016, http://www.achievement.org/achiever/wendy-kopp/, accessed July 14, 2018.

7. "Wendy Kopp" in "120 Women Who Changed Our World," Kara Ladd, *Good Housekeeping*, March 2, 2018, https://www.goodhousekeeping .com/life/inspirational-stories/g2239/women-who-changed-our -world/?slide=12, accessed July 14, 2018.

8. "Wangari Maathai—Biographical," *Nobelprize.org*. Nobel Media AB 2014, http://www.nobelprize.org/nobel_prizes/peace /laureates/2004/maathai-bio.html, accessed July 14, 2018.

9. Sheena McKenzie, "7 Women Who Changed the World," *CNN*, March 2, 2015, www.cnn.com/2015/03/02/world/7-women-who-changed -the-world/index.html, accessed July 14, 2018.

10. "Wangari Maathai—Biographical."

11. "Harriet Beecher Stowe," *History.com*, A&E Television Networks, 2009, www.history.com/topics/harriet-beecher-stowe, accessed July 14, 2018.

12. J. Lee Grady, "12 Trail-Blazing Christian Women You Should Celebrate," *Charisma Magazine*, March 2, 2016, www.charismamag.com/blogs /fire-in-my-bones/25741-12-trail-blazing-christian-women-you-should -celebrate, accessed July 14, 2018.

13. Ibid.

She DREAMS

DIG DEEP INTO THE LIFE OF MOSES TO FIND YOUR OWN GOD-GIVEN DREAMS

With the *She Dreams: Live the Life You Were Created For* companion study guide and DVD, explore the life of Moses in a six-week study experience. From his birth in Egypt to his life in the wilderness, Moses' story reveals how God calls, equips, and trains us to pursue the dreams He plants within our hearts. The study guide includes everything needed for a group study, including five personal lessons for each week, guided video notes, group discussion questions, and tips for leaders. The DVD offers video featuring Tiffany's authentic and engaging teaching style with six 20–25 minute sessions.

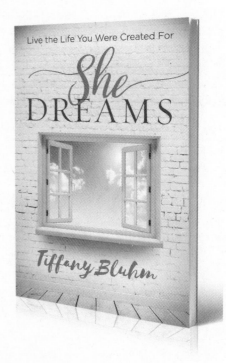

DVD | 9781501878367 | $49.99

Study Guide with Leader Helps | 9781501878343 | $12.99

Find samples at AbingdonWomen.com.

Also from
Tiffany Bluhm

In the *Never Alone* Bible study, Tiffany invites us to find healing for our hurts as we experience the unfailing companionship of Jesus. This six-week study reveals the healing power of Jesus' unconditional love through encounters He had with six hurting women in the Gospels: the woman caught in adultery, hemorrhaging woman, woman at the well, woman who anointed Him, Mary Magdalene, and Mary, Jesus' mother.

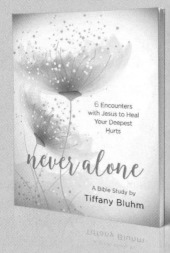

6 Encounters with Jesus to Heal Your Deepest Hurts

never alone

A Bible Study by
Tiffany Bluhm

Never Alone: 6 Encounters with Jesus to Heal Your Deepest Hurts
Bible Study Components

Participant Workbook | 9781501845826   Leader Guide | 9781151845840
DVD | 9781501845864   Leader Kit | 9781501845871

Never Alone: Exchanging Your Tender Hurts for God's Healing Grace
Book | 9781501848636

Find Samples at AbingdonWomen.com

Available Wherever Books are Sold.

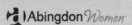

Abingdon *Women*